FATHER

FORGIVE THEM

The Four Laws Of Forgiveness

FATHER
FORGIVE THEM
The Four Laws Of Forgiveness

*Memories of Survival during
WWII in Nazi Germany*

ROSEMARIE REINHARD MUSSO

Xulon Press

Xulon Press
2301 Lucien Way #415
Maitland, FL 32751
407.339.4217
www.xulonpress.com

Cover Design by: Christine Musso Bruce.

Printed in the United States of America.

ISBN-13: 9781545611395

READER RESPONSE AND REFLECTIONS

*A*s I reflected on Rosemarie's book, some of my past experiences overlapped. She lived near Fulda, Germany, the area our war planes focused on during the cold war. Her path to forgive Hitler was similar to my path to forgive Jane Fonda (although, admittedly, Hitler's crimes were of a different order of magnitude). Her admiration for her father as a great leader (which I define as "one who leads after death") and her passion to extend his legacy through her own actions and influence on her daughters and all those who read her story makes me smile as I remember my father and seek to enrich his legacy. I felt a kinship with her as I read her scholarly tome.

Rosemarie professes the profound secrets of contentment in living through serving others and embracing forgiveness as an act of will while asking God to complete the healing process. She aptly presents forgiveness as a spiritual weapon to destroy the enemy. The book oozes wisdom nuggets, such as battles are opportunities to prove what you believe, God has your back, and the fear of God is stronger than fear of man.

To me, she is one of God's angels, taking the scars she bore from her World War II childhood and tough acclimation to her new life in the United States and translating it into an instructive and scholarly work that reads with ease and makes sense rationally for how forgiveness is such an extraordinary tool toward enlarging one's capacity to love. I was blessed to get to know her through the power of her words. Give yourself that same blessing.

—Colonel C. H. "Stretch" Dunn

Rosemarie Reinhard Musso's memoir is an authentic record of her family's experiences under Hitler's dictatorial regime that included drama and tragedy and resulted in a death sentence to all members of her family for aiding and helping prisoners of war and forced labor workers from different countries.

The book is well documented and researched, and evidence is abundantly presented to support the author's position.

The author skillfully tackles many issues from the Christian perspective, and her narration is superb. The book is a real page-turner and grabs the reader's attention from the very first page. Musso's credentials as a licensed attorney, guardian ad litem, certified mediator, and licensed and ordained minister make her well qualified for this superbly crafted memoir.

Musso chronicles in detail grand events that were inscribed in the history annals with golden letters. Musso's insider account is a second-to-none testimony, accurate, captivating, compelling, and stands alone in the crowded field of memoirs.

—Peter Kirchikov
Author
Walnuts on My Bookshelf:
Memories of Living in Communist Russia and
World War Two Encyclopedic Dictionary

Rosemarie so beautifully takes us inside her life and what it was like to live in Germany during Hitler's reign of terror. It was one of the most horrific times in modern history, and we, from Rosemarie's experience, learn not only the depravity of man, but we also see the joy of forgiveness.

Father, Forgive Them will be a great aid and blessing to those who are struggling with forgiving others.

Rosemarie certainly strikes a chord as she demonstrates through her life the forgiveness Jesus himself had when He said, "Father, forgive them" (Luke 23:34).

"If you are suffering from a bad man's injustice, forgive him lest there be two bad men" (Augustus).

May God bless you as you both learn and apply Rosemarie's Four Laws of Forgiveness.

—Dr. Mike Rouse
Sr. Pastor, Mountain View Baptist Church
President, American Association of Christian Schools

A strong story written by a strong woman—yet at the heart of her story is grace and mercy and love. If you have any disappointments in your life, I recommend this book for healing and encouragement.

—Honorable J. Gary Pate
Circuit Court Judge
Tenth Judicial Circuit of Alabama

DEDICATION

*I*n loving memory of my father, Richard Reinhard, Zahnarzt (Dentist; 1893–1991), for his strong faith and dedication not only to his family during World War II (WWII) but also to the Jewish people and POWs (prisoners of war). My father, as a result of Hitler's dictatorship indeed exposed himself to all of the Fuehrer's evil plots during the Third Reich, thus leaving him unprotected and defenseless to the ever-present, great dangers of war and an oppressive regime. Regardless of the dire circumstances, he kept helping Jews and war prisoners. I truly believe that because of his never-ending trust in his Heavenly Father, God was looking out for him and protected him during these perilous times. My father helped countless number of Jews and POWs during the Nazi Regime and was instrumental in saving Jewish lives from certain death. He was one of the unsung heroes of WWII and will always be my hero.

In 2011, my father was recognized as a *Righteous Gentile* by the Holocaust Museum, Yad Vashem, in Jerusalem. What an honor!

Also in loving memory of my mother, Kornelia Weismantel Reinhard, for her continued encouragement and strong backbone and wisdom during the toughest times during WWII. I want to leave a legacy of both helping people, like my father, which he exemplified during WWII and likewise walk in the God-given wisdom my mother exhibited. No matter what dangers to which my parents were exposed, even when our lives were at risk, my mother's inspiring God-given wisdom helped my father to develop resistance in the crucible circumstances of war. He never gave up and never bowed his knee to Hitler. God always protected my father and his family, and he lived to be ninety-seven years old. Surely, he enjoyed the favor of God.

I want to thank my daughters, Barbara E. McCoy and Christine Musso Bruce, for their continued love and support toward all of my goals. I thank God for my sweet daughters each and every day. Barbara and Christine, you never gave up on me or my project, encouraged me, and were my cheerleaders through all my struggles and success. I love you with all my heart. I am so proud of you, Barbara and Christine, for the wonderful, thoughtful, gracious, and very special ladies you have become. Christine, thank you for both your insight and using your talent for the beautiful design you created for the book cover which is absolutely stunning. Barbara, thank you for your excellent brainstorming and adding your ideas and finishing touches to the outcome of this project. A big thank you to you both for your positive support, enhancements and contribution to my book. I love you both very, very much, always.

In memory of my dear friend, Lance Watkins, who proofread and selflessly prayed while in the midst of his fight with cancer before he went on to be with his Lord, as well as my dear friend, Michaelle McGinnis, who helped in the birthing process of my endeavor to write this book.

Also a big thanks to my dear friend, Susan Forsyth, for her insight and help in promoting my story with Total Living Network (TLN) in Chicago, Moody Institute, and Wheaton College, as well as her continued encouragement.

Also a big thanks to my dear friend, Denise Goodson, who edited my manuscript and for her expertise and knowledge of grammar. She has an eagle eye and calls herself the Grammar Police. Thanks, Denise, for your hard work.

Also a big thank you to my dear friend Peter Kirchikov, Author of *Walnuts on my Bookshelf,* who resourcefully used his talents and knowledge to perfect the finishing touches of my book, writing the author's bio, and otherwise helping with his expertise and know-how to bring alive memories of growing up under Hitler.

I also want to thank Cheryl Mathews and the Republican Women of Trussville, as well as Frances Taylor, President, Alabama Federation of Republican Women (AFRW), who encouraged me throughout this process and also helped by promoting this project, as well as all of my other dear friends and prayer warriors who never quit encouraging me and kept praying for me. Thank you always.

Given my circumstances of growing up during WWII, I have had decades to process and heal from all the memories and pain I endured while growing up in Nazi Germany. Only now have I come to realize that God Himself saved my entire family from early death due to my father's tireless efforts in aiding the Jews and POWs during this horrific time in history. Because of God's blessings upon my family, I will always be grateful to my father, Richard Reinhard.

And always, to God be the glory.

ABOUT THE AUTHOR

*R*osemarie Reinhard Musso was born and raised in Germany during World War II and witnessed first-hand the atrocities and tragedies of the Third Reich during Hitler's reign. She was second to the youngest in a family of eight siblings.

Although only a child at the time, she has vivid memories of survival during World War II (WWII) in Nazi Germany, which she shares in her poignant memoir *Father, Forgive Them: The Four Laws of Forgiveness*.

The Reinhard family lived in the village of Sterbfritz in Hessen, Germany. The small idyllic, beautiful, and serene village was located near the southern mountains of Germany, close to Bavaria, where her father, Richard Reinhard, practiced dentistry in the rural area of Sterbfritz as well as surrounding villages. A coal mine was located nearby where the slave laborers, POWs (prisoners of war), and Jews from West and East European countries, Belgium, Holland, and France, were forced to work. Per regulations, the Nazis brought the workers who had serious dental problems to Dr. Reinhard's office, which was located in their family home.

Dentist Reinhard and his family had big hearts, compassion, and love for the POWs and slave workers and provided not only much-needed dental services but also gave them food, showed compassion, and treated them in a humane and civilized manner, unheard of at that time in WWII Germany. Unfortunately, since this was against the official policies of the Third Reich and Hitler's regime, their kindness initiated constant daily and obstructive surveillance by Hitler's vicious and murderous secret police, the Gestapo and SS troops on all of the Reinhard family and placed them on the special index of the "undesirables," "disloyals," "traitors," and "enemies of the nation," that is, "enemies of the Third Reich," and was ready to execute them with the country's laws of the war time. Atrocities of Hitler's regime knew no limits and resulted in a sentence to execute Dentist Reinhard in Danzig, Germany.

Luckily, it was destiny's smile that Dentist Reinhard had a patient, a baroness, who at one time was a governess in the household of Kaiser Wilhelm. The baroness suffered from a gum disease, and Dentist Reinhard was the only dentist in Germany or Switzerland who was able to help her. The baroness had a close friend, a highly posted general in Hitler's war machine at Hitler's headquarters in Hanau, Germany. She pleaded with the general, as a personal favor to her, not to execute the only dentist who was able to help her with this gum disease. Within hours, the family's fate was changed by orders from Berlin headquarters to Hanau not to execute her dentist. He was spared from ever having to appear in Danzig. God had a ram in the bush.

Hitler did not stop there, and eventually the date for the whole family's execution by hanging was legally set. Hitler's regime was ready to hang Dentist Reinhard and his family when the American Army troops came to occupy their village. After being informed by the villagers that the Reinhard family was about to be hung, the troops speedily rushed to their home and managed to liberate them only a few hours before the scheduled execution. Dentist Reinhard and his family have always been grateful to the United States and its troops for liberating them and saving their lives.

In 1959, Rosemarie Reinhard Musso married a US Army Officer and moved to Birmingham, Alabama, in 1961 where she has lived ever since with her two daughters, Barbara and Christine. She worked hard in her new adopted country to live the American dream, and she succeeded by going back to school and getting the best education she could, learning English, excelling at her job with different law firms, and volunteering with local TV productions. She is proud to have received her law degree in 2006 and is very proud of that accomplishment to fulfill her dream of practicing law.

Rosemarie Reinhard Musso is a devout Christian and is proud of her two daughters and four grandchildren. Her hobbies are art, music, and horses.

Her book, *Father, Forgive Them: The Four Laws of Forgiveness,* is the result of her unique life experience.

Peter Kirchikov
Author
*Walnuts on My Bookshelf: Memories
of Living in Communist Russia* and
World War Two Encyclopedic Dictionary

CONTENTS

INTRODUCTION

*H*ow many times do we get angry with someone or become disgruntled about something during the course of just one day? Offenses are coming against us on a daily basis—some more, some less—but they will come. The world as well as the body of Christ, including myself, has had a hard time in dealing with forgiveness. Why is it so hard to forgive? Why is it so hard to overcome tribulation, pain, suffering, or rejection? We just don't have any answers to some of the trials, but to some we do. I think the most important thing to remember while being tested is to realize that opposition and trials build character; that's exactly what Jesus is looking for in our lives: character, integrity, patience, and most of all *love* and *compassion*. It's never easy; just don't give up.

Facing problems can turn us either into a victim if we accept them as handicaps or a victor if we look at our mountains of adversity as a challenge rather than a hindrance. Certainly, this famous quote has remained true: *A winner never quits, and a quitter never wins.*

It is important for us to understand that if we would just yield to God and allow Him to break us, we could negate a lot of our problems. God longs for us to be in harmony with Him. We have to get out of our spiritual wheelchairs and start climbing the mountains of opportunity. With God's help, we can do it.

I came to the United States in 1961 with my husband and our young daughter, Barbara, who was nine months old at that time. What a special day--I finally arrived in America, the land of opportunity.

However, soon after my arrival in the United States, I realized that I was only speaking high school English (King's English). After this realization, I went into panic mode. My mind kept on racing about all the things for which I was not prepared. I had to face reality. Immediately, I knew that I would surely have to climb some ominous mountains which were now staring at me in a whole new world. Would I be able to climb them? Hesitantly, I told myself, "Yes, you will," and "Yes, you can do this."

From the very first day I set foot on American soil, I realized I was in a special place, a place where even a young female from a foreign country could go as far and climb as high as her talents and willingness to work could take her; that it was a place that could never fail because it had a national government that understood its role as servant rather than master of the people. I never would have dreamed that one day I would be actually practicing law in the United States.

On my road to success, I learned the importance of making choices to overcome difficult circumstances and afflictions and want to share with you some important factors to help you overcome the consequential pain and anguish.

Obstacles are designed from blocking us to reach our goals—our dreams. They come in different forms. I also want to share overcoming difficult circumstances and hardships, such as I experienced as a child during WWII in Nazi Germany—more specifically, the tough and testing times our family experienced during Hitler's horrendous and deadly regime. Yes, we must never forget.

My experiences of growing up under Hitler as well as the tremendous sacrifices my father made to help Jews and war prisoners during WWII will forever be imprinted in my mind. However, no matter what dire circumstances I experienced, it prepared me to eventually fulfill my goals and taught me to persevere. This story is both for young and old.

Regardless of age, we must always be aware of the dangers facing a nation when an oppressive government headed by a tyrant—like Hitler—completely disregards God, human life, liberty, happiness, and freedom for all people. It is for that reason I want you, the reader, to know what it was like to live under the power of a regime exercising totalitarianism where mercy does not exist. It is extinct—nonexistent. Leniency and benevolence had been silenced by a cruel, brutal, and power-driven authority through dictatorship. You may ask why the German people would simply succumb to such dictatorship.

Why? Simply because people did not speak up. No one responded to the red flags, which became apparent during the sudden rise of power by Hitler after World War II (WWII).

People remained silent. That is the saddest part. What was the result of a people who stayed silent? The Holocaust. The enemy's strategies and his ruthless—and often hidden—tactics started to take place. It seemed like a small fire being kindled at first, but soon exploded into the most all-consuming blaze, barbaric slaughter and ultimately plunging into the deep darkness of evil known to man. By then, it was too late to speak up. It was too late. What deception!

I certainly did not want to forgive Hitler. How do you forgive a monster? Completely unknown to me at that time, God had the answer for me years later, but it was by way of Damascus. You may ask, *why forgive?* Did you know that unforgiveness is one of the root problems that prevents us from overcoming impediments and hardships and will open the door for all kinds of adversities, resulting in disastrous consequences? Why? It is because we are violating one of God's most important principles—to forgive. We find it easier to blame someone or blame our circumstances rather than to take responsibility for our part in a crisis or by refusing to forgive others and just blame them. We simply play the blaming game. This is not a new game. It started with Adam in Genesis in the Garden of Eden. Do you recall Adam is in essence telling God, "God this is not my fault, it's that wife *you* gave me? It's *your* fault."

This is still true today. How often do we cry out, "Oh God, why did you let this happen? Oh, this is all your fault." Maybe you are waving an accusing finger at your husband, wife, or someone else, blaming them for your calamities. If we are not careful, we can drown in our own sorrows and despair, blaming God, your spouse, your boss, and on and on.

Forgiveness is the turning point—the place in God where you have to learn how to overcome hardships, whether they are spiritual, financial, emotional, or physical. Learn to forgive and not blame God or anybody else. Remember that God never promised us a rose garden. This is part of our existence called life. Life can be cruel and full of disappointments and tragedy, but we can learn from these hard times and gain strength if we rely on God to help us with these obstacles and uncertainties, which are certain to raise their ugly heads during life. We must, however, do it God's way. This was a hard lesson for me to learn.

You see, overcoming frightful and dire circumstances is *coming over* to God's side of doing things. We can't be overcomers unless we do it God's way, and if we don't learn to forgive, problems will only boomerang. Remember, to overcome is to come over to the other side—God's side. Is there a way out? Yes, absolutely. No matter how old or how young you are or how much trouble you are in, there is a way out. The bottom line is this: You must *trust* Jesus Christ. Simply trust Him. Experientially, I know He will see you through, no matter how complex your problems may be. Yes, it may not be easy, but it works.

We must simply believe. What is believing? Believing is trusting in the reality of Jesus; not with your mind *but with your heart*. Believing is a *knowing* deep down inside your soul that if you really trust and rely on Him, you will make it. Trust is always a big issue. If you truly trust God like a child, you will know that whatever you are going through is a test and a place where He works out some things *in* you rather than doing things *for* you.

Undoubtedly, you will know that you will pass the test. In order to have this knowledge, we have to be grounded in the Word, but how? As you study the Word of God, it will take root in you and withstand the test of time. This fundamental trust in God will get rid of all your fears, doubts, worry, and unbelief because you finally realize that there is absolutely nothing you can do about your situation, not in your own strength anyway. Trust will plant that inner confidence and peace that you are going to be all right. It will give you the strength to overcome any obstacle. We can never just fake trust—either we trust Jesus or we don't. Because of my strict upbringing and growing up during the war, I have always had a big trust issue with God. I would pretend to trust him and try to fake it, but that never worked. It took years for me to finally be able to really trust God. He will help us get to that place of total surrender and trust. However, it took some time.

I pray that the Holy Spirit will enlighten you and that you will embrace the way your Father chooses to bring you to a point of surrender to Him, whatever road that may be. I took the long route by way of Damascus. I certainly would not recommend this route. We need to realize that His ways are not our ways. While we look at our circumstances, especially while we are drowning in pain and despair, we need to remember that

God looks at the finished product. But guess what. It is like being on the potter's wheel. The potter clearly sees beforehand and already has a vision of the beautiful work he is about to create, although the object on the wheel doesn't realize that it is being prepared for a useful purpose and for beauty.

It is while being on the potter's wheel that the beauty of the artwork is being fashioned. Of course, it remains on the potter's wheel until the artist achieves the desired shape he or she has previously envisioned. Next, after the heat has reached the desired degree and before placing the article very carefully in the fiery furnace, the potter applies glaze to the clay to seal in all the rough spots. Finally, after quite a lengthy process, the article comes out of the fire. However, the vessel may once more be placed in the oven under intense heat, maybe even several more times—until it is flawless. This procedure is repeated until the potter is satisfied, and perfection is achieved—ouch! The potter then puts the finishing touches on his product and behold; now it radiates and glories in its beauty.

God uses the same process with us. At times, we seem to forget that God is the potter and we are the clay. Be mindful that the more we yield to the pressure in the fire, the quicker the work is done. Remember, *no one* just *loves* to go through the fire. Don't forget, you can't be both the potter and the clay. Let God be God, and let the clay be clay, ready to be molded into what the potter desires the clay to be.

Be encouraged.

1

THE WAR BEGINS

Satan's Strategies

"*G*et off my back, Bozo, I'm tired of this."

"I'm tired of you, too."

Slam-slam-slam-Bang. Pictures on the wall slightly move to the side as the walls are being shaken by the slam of the door. Tears are streaming. Pulses are racing at high speed—like an electric percolator—and purple blood vessels are bulging out of the skin as if to explode as a fist lands on the table.

You exclaim, "Oh, God, I can't stand this anymore. I've had enough. I just can't take it anymore."

By now, a deadly silence is settling in. No further exchange of words, no sounds are heard except for small sobs slowly releasing the anger and hurt felt from the deepest innermost being within the two, thereby releasing an atmosphere of hostility, war, and depression in the home. Does this scenario bring back memories?

Maybe you are hurting because of harsh words hurled at you, or you feel the pain resulting from a broken relationship with your children, your spouse, or maybe a friend. Are you hurting now because someone you love has grieved you, hurt you, deserted you, spoke all manner of evil against you, told lies about you, or was ungrateful and just utterly broke your heart? Maybe it was a broken promise. Someone you trusted let you down and did not keep their word.

Maybe your child rebelled against you by choosing a life-style contrary to what the Word of God teaches or rebelled against your standards, which you set for them as well as your-self, and now, your heart is so shattered that you don't think you can bear it.

God Makes a Way of Escape

If you are asking for relief, let me tell you where and how you can find it. Do you need to forgive someone? Read on. Forgiveness is like medicine for our souls; it heals our emo-tional scars from the wounds and brokenness, which very often remain hidden in the depth of our hearts.

Most of the time, we try to bury these offenses in our sub-conscious. Whether we need emotional or physical healing, we have to ask God to reveal to us all our hidden struggles and pain. To enable us to receive healing, God will expose—as a matter of certainty—plug up, and root out all our lingering hurts with which we have tried to wrestle, but without suc-cess. This healing process takes time for most of us; it's not an instant fix. Yes, it takes time. Most importantly, in order to retain our healing, we absolutely have to be equipped with the fruit of the Holy Spirit: "Love, joy, peace, longsuffering, gentleness, goodness, faith, meekness, temperance: against such there is no law" (Galatians 5:22–23).

We must allow God to work these fruits out inside of us, which is a growing process to strengthen us to follow God in obedience to His laws; thus, we will not be left vulnerable to Satan, the enemy of our soul. This is the season in our lives where God wants to do things *in* us rather than asking God to do things *for* us.

This is also our "pruning" process, also known as sanctification, to grow and mature from small seeds into trees of righteousness—from a baby in Christ to full maturity in Christ. Sometimes, time itself may be a healer. It is very important that we allow ourselves time to heal. Healing can only take place, though, if we do it God's way and only God's way. Obedience is the key. God gives us the key and enables us to walk in forgiveness, but He leaves it up to us to use the key and keep the door open so that forgiveness will rule in our heart. How do we obey God? Remember what the mother of Jesus, Mary, told the disciples at the wedding? "Whatever he says to you, do it" (John 2:5). When the steward asked for wine, and Jesus asked the disciples to fill the empty pots with water, it didn't make sense to them, but they obeyed. Likewise, just as the mother of Jesus advised—do what he says. *Follow His plan*: His will, His word, and His ways.

To learn and know His plan may take some time. This depends on how flexible we are to listen and be obedient to

His plan. Let me take you back on my journey from the battle scars and hopelessness of WWII to a place of refreshing, an oasis and shelter of restoration and healing of my heart and soul. It is a place where you can find peace in the midst of the storms of life—in the lion's den or fiery furnace. Remember, offenses will come. However, we have to be prepared and know *how* to deal with and respond to them.

If we choose to forgive, we will escape the traps of Satan to keep us bound up with our various afflictions. Have you ever wondered why the anger you have toward some people is much greater than others, even though the offense may be the same? I believe that the degree of anguish (sometimes in the form of anger) we experience depends in large part on the source from which the poisonous arrows strike our hearts. What could be the source? Oftentimes, when other believers let us down or violate us, it affects us far greater than wrongs endured against us by family members, a loved one, a friend, or merely a stranger.

We have learned or conditioned ourselves to tolerate offensive behaviors from family members or certain relationships we encounter from time to time. Primarily, the reason for this is that our expectancy level, especially as a new believer as to character and integrity toward *other* Christians is much higher. We develop a different standard between family and sometimes even friends, mostly because of the familiarity of our relationships as well as higher tolerance for failures. How often do we hear, "I love her or him, but he or she will never change," and we eventually give up and just accept and tolerate them just the way they are. However, this is not so true with "a new" believer. A new believer expects certain standards for all Christians, especially after encountering mature Christians—or role models.

Aren't Christians supposed to walk in love? Are they not supposed to forgive? What about being Christ-like? What about keeping your word—your promises to others?

Yes, these are the most difficult obstacles to overcome. A new believer assumes that *all* people who say they are "Christians" to follow the "Golden Rule," not realizing that just because they say they are a Christian does not mean they walk in maturity or have the much-needed discernment or training required to walk in the truth of the Gospel. This is a growing process from a baby in Christ to adulthood. Remember that Jesus told us that we shall know true believers by the fruit they bear. Of course, as "baby" Christians, we are in the beginning stages of learning and preparation into maturity. Much to our dismay, as new believers, we do not have this knowledge, and sometimes it may take some time for us to get this revelation. We are learning to be patient throughout the groundwork God is doing inside of us during these developmental stages.

PERSONAL NOTES

_____

_____

_____

_____

_____

_____

_____

_____

_____

_____

_____

_____

_____

_____

_____

_____

_____

_____

_____

_____

_____

_____

_____

_____

_____

_____

_____

_____

_____

2

A VISIT BACK TO GERMANY

My Father, Dentist Richard Reinhard

"*O*h, I wish I were eighty again." This was a typical expression from my father after he reached the age of eighty-five. He never lost his sense of humor even when he celebrated his eighty-fifth birthday.

I will never forget celebrating my father's eighty-fifth birthday party in the private dining room of the majestic looking castle of one of his patients and friend, a baroness. It was awesome. The table setting was a sight to behold. The lustrous and beautiful chandelier shining and reflecting its sparkle on the dark oak wooden walls and ceiling of the dining room displayed the masterful artwork exhibited throughout the castle. The eye-catching stained-glass windows contributed to the serene and magnificent atmosphere. The table was decorated in honor of my father's birthday and was fit for a king. It was magical.

Later that night, we were fortunate to continue to celebrate his birthday in a special room decorated in its baroque-style splendor which was especially designated downstairs on the bottom floor of the castle where dinner was served. The excitement by each and every one present seemed to heighten while the sound of waltz music, played by our village band, saturated this beautiful and elegant room and penetrated the walls of the castle throughout the night with the sensational and marvelous sound of Mozart's waltz music. Of course, the band could not forget the fabulous polka.

What an unforgettable, wonderful celebration — something I will never forget. This event is still deeply engraved in my mind. Although the baroness was already deceased, she granted my father permission prior to her death that during my father's lifetime, we would be allowed to celebrate special occasions in her castle. It was utterly breathtaking. My father was greatly honored, and numerous articles about my father's heroic actions were remembered in German newspapers.

One of these articles I translated for the readers as follows:

DENTIST REINHARD 85 YEARS OLD

Zeitlofts-Sterbfritz. It is unbelievable when you see this vital man that: Dentist Richard Reinhard is 85 years old. He is still practicing in Zeitlofts two times a week and is still faithfully committed to his clientele, who has been loyal to him for many long years. Dr. Herbert Meyerdierks congratulated him in the name (or on behalf) of the Dental Association of Unterfranken, and the Dental Association in the old District of Bad Brückenau and gave thanks to Richard Reinhard for being at the disposal of the patients and their dental needs for several decades, especially in the rural area.

"I wish I were 80 again," says Richard Reinhard, who keeps himself fit through his Kneipp fitness programs and his care and love for his well-groomed garden.

Richard Reinhard was born in Dietershahn, near Fulda, spent some time as part of his dental education in Petersburg, Russia, and finally established himself in Sterbfritz. Since 1969, Reinhard has been practicing in his dental office in Zeitlofs. [Translated by Rosemarie Reinhard Musso]

I remember celebrating my younger sister's wedding in the castle. Every time my thoughts wander to the awesome and awe-inspiring times we experienced in the castle of the baroness, whether a wedding or a birthday party or maybe just visiting and strolling through the park, my heart just swells up with joy about these special memories. What impressed me the most about the baroness, even as a child, was her charm and gracious demeanor. I loved her affectionate expressions of caring not only toward me, but toward others as well. What a beautiful and charming lady she was. Notably, she certainly was a true friend to my father and, eventually, instrumental in saving my father's life.

Let me tell you just a little background about my dad. Amsterdam, Holland, and St. Petersburg were the training grounds for my father to study dentistry. He spent quite some time in Holland as an intern and further interned in Russia prior to receiving his dental degree. However, much to his dismay, he had to return to Germany because he suffered from a severe illness and ultimately settled down in Fulda, Germany, which was his hometown—the same town where I graduated from high school.

He started out at a very young age as a dentist's assistant, but because of the experience and vast knowledge he had acquired in dentistry in Holland and Russia, it did not take very long for his practice to become well-known and established. As part of his internship, he was required to periodically visit and practice in numerous surrounding small towns or villages. One of them was Sterbfritz.

He never dreamed that he would eventually settle down in Sterbfritz, Sinntal, Germany and still would be practicing dentistry there at eighty-five. Having lived through the most agonizing and terrifying pain and anguish, especially during WWII, he achieved his dream.

See the article on the next page from a German Newspaper, followed by the translation.

A newspaper in Fulda, Germany, published an article "Still Practicing Dentistry," in 1978.

ARTICLE IN THE "FULDAER ZEITUNG"
Friday, June 23, 1978
(Newspaper Article in the *Fulda News*)

STILL PRACTICING DENTISTRY

Dentist Richard Reinhard is celebrating his 85th Birthday

Sinntal-Sterbfritz. This Friday Dentist Richard Reinhard is celebrating his 85th birthday. The jubilee, who is still today maintaining a practice in Zeitlofs, was born in Dietershahn. First of all, Reinhard was educated in a Holland monastery (high school) but had to return to Germany and his hometown after a severe illness where he completed his education. As a young dentist's assistant, beginning from the town of Fulda, Reinhard was required to periodically visit and practice in seven different small towns and villages, one of which was Sterbfritz. On January 15, 1919, after the First World War, in which Reinhard served on the Western front, he established himself in Sterbfritz and opened up his own dental office. During the Nazi Regime, which the honoree describes as the worst time of his life, Reinhard was especially noted during this time because of his heroic deeds toward the Jews and forced-labor prisoners.

Max Dessauer collaborated to this effect in his article, "Courage for doing a Good Deed"—Memories of Unsung Heroes" that was published in 1962 about the dentist from Sterbrtitz. Prisoners from concentration camps, who had been forced to hard labor in a nearby quarry, were brought to Reinhard because of the much-needed and necessary demand for dental care. Reinhard dispensed food to them, which he had stored in his basement for their survival.

Richard Reinhard is able to celebrate his birthday in Sterbfritz together with his surviving eight out of nine children.

His wife, with whom he was still able to celebrate their Golden Wedding Anniversary in 1973, is now deceased. [Translated by Rosemarie Reinhard Musso]

On January 15, 1919, after serving on the Western front during World War I, my father decided to settle down in Sterbfritz, Germany. My father purchased our home in this small village, which would later become a safe shelter for many, many Jews and POWs during WWII. Once Hitler came to power, opposition facing my father was imminent. My father's increasing concern was Hitler's sudden rise to power and his growing personality, mesmerizing young and old without anyone speaking out against him.

Hitler created an atmosphere of fear and terror, which would include anyone speaking out against him. You may wonder what brought Hitler to such unlimited power. It was mostly because of his eloquence of speech and apparent charm he exhibited while he spoke, and therefore, he drew in large crowds who vowed to obey him, no matter what. How clever!

Did anyone dare to speak out against Hitler? Absolutely not. People remained silent. No one dared to oppose him or speak out against him because it would mean facing imminent death. Fear was Hitler's mode of operation. It was too late to speak up. By now, Hitler's reign of suppression had already made its mark.

My father's concern grew even stronger when my brother was forced to join the Hitler Youth. The people in our village became unrecognizable in their thoughts and behaviors, as though they were complete strangers, especially toward Jewish people and war prisoners. It happened slowly, however steadily, until the realization came that your friends, at times even close friends, all of a sudden turned into your foes. What a change!

My father's response to these developments was to make sure that his children understood the danger of consolidated political power and the importance of helping the downtrodden. Additionally, adding to my father's demise, the villagers in Sterbfritz and surrounding villages at that time were mostly Protestants, and my father was the first Catholic to ever take up residence in our small village and to open his dental office there. It was hard.

During the Nazi regime, my father stood in opposition to the great European powers, but great, unshakable faith in God, together with his determination to protect his family, kept him from bowing his knee to Hitler. My father was one of the unsung heroes of WWII. I hope that his story will touch your heart as it has touched the hearts of others in the past.

Childhood Memories

Early in life I learned that *success doesn't just happen, but you set it in motion.*[1] I learned from my father, who faced many, many obstacles, that opposition gives birth to opportunity,[2] no matter how hard or impossible the task may seem. God used these hardships to shape, mold, and strengthen me so that I could overcome future hardships and obstacles, which were, of course, designed as deterrents to hinder me to follow my dreams. I always had big dreams, but I never once consulted God about them. As a certainty, my dreams never measured up to what God had planned for me because I limited myself about what I could accomplish. For example, going to law school, for me, was always going to remain *just a dream.* Was I ever surprised that God had a different plan and much bigger dreams for me than I could ever imagine, and, my dear friend, He is the only one who can bring your dreams to pass and enable and equip you to succeed.

From experience, I know firsthand the emotional damage that is always war's legacy. My childhood was filled with memories of war, hate, loneliness, food rationings resulting in hunger and starvation, and strict curfews, as well as the eerie sirens followed by loud and terrifying, noisy bombings.

Though I was a child, the memories of those war-torn years are indelibly stamped in my mind. Our family lived in a small village near the border of Southern Germany. Our home was located right across the street from a railroad station in our picturesque, idyllic, small village near Frankfurt on Main, Germany. Our home was nestled in the midst of surrounding mountains and beautiful hills, which reflected awesome beauty, serenity, and peace—much like in a Walt Disney movie. The high school I later attended was in Fulda, Germany, a city in close proximity to our little village, which was also breathtakingly beautiful. Everywhere you walked, you would encounter the majestic-looking baroque buildings, small castles, baroque domes, restaurants, and all kinds of charming shops. After school, my friends and I would often walk downtown to a specific huge baroque mansion-like estate where part of the *Sound of Music* was filmed. This was exciting. It was almost perfect. Almost!

After my father set up his dental practice in our home, he was the only dentist in our village and provided services in all of the surrounding villages. Much to his relief, a few years later, another dentist opened his dental practice in Sterbfritz, which reduced some of the heavy workload. Now, both dentists were able to take care of the patients in our village and all of the adjacent small communities. Nonetheless, the vast number of patients still created a challenge. Anywhere from seventy-five to one hundred people per day flooded my father's office. For the most part, the tremendous number of patients on a daily basis was partially due to Hitler's enforcement of *nationalization of health care* and partially due to the vast amount of people in the surrounding villages. Yes, health care was free, but was it really? This was part of the promised *change*.

What was the result of Hitler's national health care program? Doctors' offices were already filled early in the morning to full capacity. People who needed surgery often had to wait over a year. Most people, regrettably, had to wait so long, especially those in hospitals, that they eventually were forced to succumb to their demise and died. These poor individuals never had a chance to have the necessary surgery.

You may ask, but what about the children? Healthy children were forced to join the Hitler Youth; however, if your child suffered from any physical or mental challenges or disabilities, Hitler demanded that these children be admitted to a "rehabilitation" home. While there, the parents were not allowed to visit with their loved ones for a period of six months. Just imagine, they were not even allowed to have any kind of contact with their children. However, before the six months expired, each of the parents was informed, in writing, that their child had mysteriously died. How gruesome!

You may also wonder, but *what about the elderly?* Anyone who was weak, especially women and the elderly, were extinguished. Every reprehensible act known to man took place in these hospitals. Murder was suddenly called "mercy killing."

Dental services experienced the same dilemma. Under the national health care program, dentists were restricted to a minimum of dental treatments at any one visit. As a result, most patients had to come back three months later to receive the additional dental care they so desperately needed. This could last up to one year. Oftentimes, my father treated certain emergencies at no charge to prevent further damage to his patients. People came to my father's dental practice on bicycles, in cars, walked, or took a bus. Soon my father became well known not only for his expertise in dentistry but also helping others with herbal medications, such as Dr. Kneipp's herbal or homeopathic therapy. This was to save my father and our family's lives in the years to come after Hitler came to power and during the Holocaust.

As you can imagine, the reflection of war quickly became apparent as pain, hardships, and suffering and every other evil work made its mark during the Nazi regime. Screeching sirens, and the horror and deafening sound of falling bombs, over and over again, were an everyday occurrence at that time. Also, Hitler's hatred for the Jews quickly became apparent. Since our home was located across the street from the train terminal in which a *Gasthaus* (tavern) was located, I could see and observe the trains going by each and every day. As a frightened little girl, I remember watching my Jewish friends being loaded on the railroad boxcars like animals. I cannot help but remember the fear and confusion in their eyes as they departed for their horrible destination, and some were friends with whom I used to play. I also remember the anger and resolve in my father's eyes.

Now, my father was a very tough man with a hard exterior. Furthermore, my father had the ability to carry himself with great confidence and authority, especially in the presence of the

Nazis, Hitler's Gestapo (Hitler's Secret State Police), and the SS troops who were among the most powerful and terrifying political organizations in Nazi Germany. They started out as Hitler's bodyguards and blindly followed Hitler's demands and therefore, very quickly rose to power under his regime. They also served under Hitler in the death camps. With the horrors of war all around us, this was one of the ways my father used this ability to cover his real activities, which were helping dying, tortured, and starving Jews and war prisoners. The Gestapo was able to function under Hitler's regime with limitless control, having total and far-reaching immunity and, therefore, were exempt from any judicial appeals. How scary!

When the Nazis brought the Jews to my father for dental treatment, he would make a big scene in their presence. What an actor he was! Typically, the Gestapo would take the Jews out of a nearby coal mine or quarry where they were forced to hard labor. Prior to that they had been taken out of concentration camps. The Nazis packed these poor Jews like sardines in a truck to transport them to my father's office. These Jews over time developed a certain gum disease and other dental problems because of malnutrition. When the Gestapo dropped off the emaciated Jews at our house where my father's practice was located, my father would address the Jews in front of the Gestapo. Very strongly, he would feign his contempt. In bitter tones, waving his hands in the air, he would tell the Jews that he did not want these "dirty, nasty Jews" in his waiting room; also, he did not want to mingle the Jews with his German patients.

He would then command the prisoners to go downstairs into the cellar because he would not tolerate "nasty, dirty Jews" intermingling with his patients. Convinced and approving of my father's harsh treatment and seeming disdain for the Jews, the guards would be satisfied, and with a smug glow of self-congratulation, leave the Jews to their supposed tormentor. The Nazi officers would later head off to the nearby Gasthaus (like a tavern), located within the train terminal across the street from our home to entertain themselves until it was time to come back and pick up their prisoners to transport them back to the coal mine.

Once the guards were gone, it was a different story in the Reinhard's house. Much to the prisoners' relief, they found in "that dreaded cellar" the comforts of food, clothing, and a genuine break from their real tormentors. They could strengthen themselves with some nourishment and tender care as well as medical attention to ease their pain, at least for a few hours. At that time, it was against the law to treat Jews and war prisoners. Therefore, my father was instructed not to give the Jews any anesthetic—just to pull their teeth without it. How cruel!

So long as I remember, my father was always very proud of his very special vegetable garden. During this time, a Jewish attorney with his skeleton-like small frame came in our garden where my father grew lettuce, onions, leeks, and so forth. His weary-looking eyes were hollow, and he appeared to be starving to death. Clearly, I can remember the pleading look he had when he asked my father if he could have just one of his leeks. His look was a look of total despair and hopelessness.

He silently motioned to the garden and said, "I am so hungry. Dr. Reinhard, can I have just one of your leeks?"

My father replied, "No, you cannot have just one leek, but you can fill your pockets full and put lettuce or anything else you want in your pockets."

To keep from starving to death, the Jews would hide these commodities from their oppressors inside the lining of their coats. Of course, my father made it clear to the Jews and POWs that they would always have access to his vegetable garden. How sad!

What about freedom of religion? Was there freedom of religion? Absolutely not. We were under surveillance, and Nazi soldiers would spy on us and would register times and dates when we could go to church until such time as they made church attendance impossible by ordering my father to see patients on Sunday morning. Thus they made sure that he would not attend church on Sundays on a regular basis. When, on some occasions, he did sneak away and go to church, punishment was awaiting him, and his workload doubled on Sunday.

This was soon to change again. The government then ordered him to fulfill certain duties on Sunday to prevent him and his family from going to church at any time. We, of course, became aware then that there were spies everywhere.

Growing up Catholic, we had to be most careful with any religious activities. For that reason, our priest would occasionally arrive at our house in civilian clothing. My father took a lot of chances while all of the priest's official garments were secretly hidden in my parents' bedroom, and whenever a safe moment presented itself, the priest secretly held mass or taught bible study at our home, without the priestly garments, of course. Eventually, public mass in church was replaced by Hitler with mandatory physical education, thereby making it impossible to attend church on Sunday ever again. God was no longer welcome anywhere, including, but not limited to, government, schools and even in the privacy of our homes. How foolish!

Since the time my father opened his dental practice, he always kept a picture of Jesus in the Garden of Gethsemane in his practice, which was located on the first floor of our home. On one occasion, as the Nazis furiously rummaged through our home, they tore the picture off the wall, put up Hitler's picture, and dared my father to take it down. Did my father obey? He had to obey their commands to keep from being shot, although he was utterly dismayed. As soon as my father was assured they had left, he switched the pictures again. Now, he was on the lookout for the Nazis, and as soon as my father saw them coming close to our home, he put Hitler's picture back up, but swapped it back after they would leave. It was tormenting not only to him but the constant turmoil affected our whole family as well.

We never knew when the Nazis would invade our home to conduct a search. Privacy in our home was unmistakably over. There was no freedom because Hitler's dictatorship demanded that if you did not follow him, death was certain. His theory was to be brutal and ruthless. Because my father helped the Jews, he was considered an enemy of the Reich. My father's activities to help the Jews was soon to be exposed.

Sadly, the Gestapo eventually found out what my father was doing. Life drastically changed. The Nazis used severe means and methods to annihilate my father as well as his family. Of course, by then people had succumbed to his power and Hitler was in total control.

At the time Hitler came to power, there was a tremendous financial depression. During the recession in Germany, people lost their homes and jobs, very similar to the Great Depression in the United States during the 1930s. Hitler promised change. Continuously, His charm and charisma as well as his eloquent speech helped him to come to power. People in Germany needed change desperately. They wanted change. However, no one would have ever imagined that this change would include the Holocaust until red flags became apparent.

But still, the people ignored the red flags. People were silent. No one would speak up, and actually, no one truly believed it. They were in denial, even up to the time when Hitler blamed the Zionists, especially Zionist bankers, for all the problems in Germany and promised that he would wipe them off the face of the earth. It is interesting to note that Hitler was a church member until the day he died. It is, therefore, understandable that Jewish people view the Holocaust, perpetrated by Christian Hitler—in the land of reformation—as a Christian phenomenon. Sadly, the church was silent. No one spoke up.

The silent hush, the stark silence of the people as well as the church, actually empowered Hitler to win. Silence equals inaction and gives rise to the power of all evil. Because no one spoke up—neither the church nor the people, the result was that rather than the people silencing evil, the church as well as the people were silenced by the dictator and suffered horrific consequences and backlashes for their silence. When government takes the wrong turn and gets off of the path which our forefathers designed and laid out as a blueprint for us, we need to *speak up* and let our voices be heard.

In 1944, a national militia called Volkssturm was established, and all males between the ages 16 to 60 were drafted to military service. My father received a subpoena (*Stellungsbefehl*) to appear in Danzig in front of the gestapo (the superior judges there at that time) where he was to be executed. By law, he had to appear. He received the subpoena on a Thursday, and he was to appear in Danzig the following Wednesday. Russians had already occupied Danzig and, consequently, my father would have been shot immediately. Gripped by sudden fear and panic-stricken, my father asked my mother, "What are we going to do?"(Aren't you glad that God created Eve for Adam?)

My mother, of course, was truly terrified and started thinking about this dilemma. That turned out to be another sleepless night for both of my parents. This was a strategic time to act with God's wisdom. Prayerfully, she decided that my father should go and see the baroness as the best immediate solution. Surely she would be able to help him.

In his despair, my father, of course, took my mother's advice and sought the help of the baroness, who also was one of his patients. Because the Nazis had already confiscated my father's automobile, he took his bicycle and with troubling thoughts, headed to the nearby beautiful and stately looking castle, Schloss Ramholz, which is still located in close proximity to our village.

Truly, God is sovereign. Filled with foreboding thoughts about his life and that of his family, would she help him?

Now, the baroness had great political clout and thus was very influential throughout Germany. She met my father because she suffered from a certain gum disease and had sought dental help both in Germany and Switzerland to no avail. She heard of my father who ended up as the only dentist in Germany who was able to help her. Her butler would bring her to my father's practice, sometimes late at night or at other odd times, whenever she was in severe pain. My father had the cure and she was very grateful.

Yes, indeed, the baroness helped him. After my father's arrival at her castle, her butler immediately led him to the baroness. Hoping against hope, he handed the baroness his subpoena and asked her, "Baroness, can you help me?"

After looking at the subpoena, her first response was, "Reinhard, you know what this means," to which my father replied, "Yes, I know; this will be the end of me and my family."

Needless to say, she confirmed my father's deep concern by slightly bowing her head, whispering, "Yes, Reinhard, that would be the end of you." Then immediately, the baroness took action as vivid memories of her dear friend, a high-ranking general at Hitler's headquarters, came to mind. "Of course," she exclaimed. "I will call my dear friend, General Walther von Brauchitsch. I know he can help you."

Without hesitation, she called him, hoping for a miracle. She pleaded with the general as a personal favor to her not to execute her dentist. She emphasized that this was her personal dentist, who was also the *only* dentist in Germany who was able to help her with a rare gum disease from which she suffered and was in desperate need of his services. This fortuitous call saved his life.

The baroness, indeed, prevailed in her plea for my father's life. Within a few hours, orders were issued from Hitler's headquarters to Hanau not to execute my father. His life was spared.

What a miracle. Who was this great general?

The general, Walther von Brauchitsch was a field marshal and Commander-in-Chief of the Wehrmacht during the early years during WWII. The general was young and well decorated with the highest honors for all his accomplishments in Germany. Regrettably, the dramatic and tragic fate of the general who saved my father's life, was as a result of the general's failure to seize Moscow. Sadly, because of this, Hitler showed his disdain toward Brauchitsch by much abuse and relieving him of his command. The general retired in December 1941, and Hitler took direct control of the Wehrmacht. However, the general was arrested and charged with war crimes. Because of the severe abuse by Hitler, his health suffered, and he passed away in 1948 before he could be prosecuted at the Nuremberg trials (Wikipedia Encyclopedia). This was brutal!

This awesome general was actually instrumental in protecting my father from the "special" Nazi forces who were determined to destroy my father by any means possible. However, because he was such a high-ranking general at that time, he actually warned the Nazis not to destroy my father and ironically, rather than persecuting him they had to protect him out of fear of the consequences they would face from the general had they harmed my father in any way. What divine, supernatural protection.

I still have vibrant and fond memories of the baroness. She not only became a close friend to my mother and father, but I always eagerly and excitedly looked forward to her visits. Often, when her husband, the baron, came with her, it always turned out to be an incredibly special occasion because of his kindness and thoughtfulness he showed toward me. Without fail, he would always put me on his lap, play, and spend time with me. I loved and treasured these unique and extraordinary times. I remember often, in anxious anticipation to the arrival of the baroness and her husband, I tirelessly practiced how to make a perfect curtsy. Yes, a curtsy. When the baroness and the baron arrived, my sisters and I were required to greet her with a curtsy, simply to show respect. I certainly did not want to mess up.

How exciting it was to see both the baroness and her husband arrive at our home. These visits always turned out to be very sensational. The baroness was very charming, beautiful, and so kind. Also, had it not been for her incredible intervention, my father would have faced certain death.

These memories are extremely special to me, as this was the closest I ever came to feeling loved as a child. In retrospect, I came to realize my father was always occupied to full capacity with his patients on a daily basis. At the same time, he was forced to constantly be on guard, with much anxiety, because of the scrutinizing surveillance, day in and day out, of all of his activities during these dreadful times. While our very existence was in danger, it seemed there was no time for showing affection. Simply surviving had become part of life.

After the miraculous victory by the general saving my father's life, the fight was not over. Although my father faced death and suffered through tremendous persecution, he continued to reach out to the Jews and war prisoners by even helping some escape by either hiding some Jews and war prisoners under our beds, in the attic or basement, or gave some war prisoners civilian clothes and, thus, helped some of the Jewish families escape to other countries like Belgium. He helped others by secretly taking care of them in our basement. Surprisingly, one of the families he helped to escape to Belgium came to see my father at our home after the war. Both my parents and the Belgium family warmly embraced each and every one of these visits, and both were grateful for the reunion for several years to come. I vividly remember their smiling faces just mentioning the name of my father, shaking their head in unbelief at his tremendous courage to help the downtrodden. They were so grateful.

Likewise, a Jewish professor, whom my father helped escape to France, returned after the war to thank my father, together with the bishop of Paris. He was not only a patient of my father, but they became friends while he lived in our little village, Sterbfritz. The Jewish professor described his gratitude in a newspaper article about my father, whom he referred to in his news article as an *unsung hero*. He also mentioned the veterinarian who, together with my father, aided a poor Jew who peddled goods in our village. They secretly aided him by peddling his goods for him to help him with his finances and supplying food and clothing to him. Sadly, though, he was one of the millions who were killed after being transported with other Jewish villagers to Dachau. How sad.

Below is a translation of an article from the Jewish professor who wrote the following in 1962:

Courage for Doing a Good Deed
Memories of an Unsung Hero

Now the time has come to celebrate memories. One remembers the good and bad occasions, but I always miss hearing about people who acted without fear, indefatigably and courageously, during the darkest periods of time. They really deserve that we remember their actions. During these years of hardship, they acted in isolation and, therefore, continuously risked their lives and that of their families. We will talk about some of these unsung heroes, as Kurt Grossman addressed them.

First of all, there is the dentist who still resides and practices in my hometown. There was a huge quarry in the close vicinity during the Nazi regime where prisoners from concentration camps were brought and condemned to forced labor until they collapsed or died, some of which were French men who were arrested by the Gestapo in France. Among them, for example, was a high Church official and, of course, a lot of Jews. The food rations and maintenance allotted these forced labor prisoners did not even meet the bare minimal standards.

They soon developed scurvy (*scorbut*) due to vitamin deficiency and as a result developed, among other symptoms, severe toothaches and gum disease, causing their teeth to fall out. They were sent to the above-mentioned dentist who, first of all, examined them and sent the prisoners into his basement which served as waiting room.

He purposely made it look like a "special" waiting room for prisoners. In reality there was a pleasant surprise waiting for them. The basement was pleasantly furnished, and the prisoners found food, heat, and cooking facilities there. They were able to stay for hours. Also their clothing and shoes were taken care of. Their guards, without complaining, enjoyed waiting in a nearby Gasthaus during that time. If they had ever found out what went on in the dentist's basement just one time, it would have led to immediate arrest and execution for the dentist and his family.

It was not always easy to provide enough food for everyone. Because most of the clientele of the dentist consisted of almost all farmers, he managed very skillfully to somehow exchange his dental services to his patients for food and other necessities. When I mention those times to him, his family, and his children today, they just motion wearily and quietly. They feel what they did was just a matter of course or to be taken for granted. However, in this manner, life for prisoners in the quarry was made considerably more bearable and tolerable, and many lives were saved because of it.

The high Church official (Bishop of Paris) lives in Paris again today in the Rue d'Assomption. Since I have lived in Paris for twenty-five years, I paid him a visit one day and was happy to hear what strong affections and happy memories he had for my hometown and especially for the dentist and his family. After the war, he returned to my hometown several times to visit the dentist and his family, which was the biggest reward of all for the dentist.

At the end I want to mention a German veterinarian who somehow moved to this village a long time ago. He did not have anything to do with the Nazis. He was working together with the aforementioned dentist but also did something else.

There was an old Jewish domestic peddler, Lazarus Hecht, who sold fly catchers, yarn, pencils, and articles of this sort, who was real poor devil, and when he was forbidden to leave the village and was not even allowed to go to the farmer's houses in the village to sell his articles, he was near death due to starvation.

The veterinarian then would have the peddler give him the fly catchers and other kinds of domestic articles several times a week and then he secretly sold them to the farmers for the peddler and brought him the money, potatoes, and other food. He might very well have been the only veterinarian in the world who peddled with fly catchers. [Translated by Rosemarie Reinhard Musso]

Hitler's pursuit of my father was not over. My father and our whole family continued to face death by continuing to help Jews and war prisoners in any way possible. Had Hitler succeeded in killing my father, our whole family would have been wiped out. Much to our amazement, my parents still celebrated their fiftieth wedding anniversary. What a hero!

Below is a translation of my father's golden wedding anniversary, which appeared in one of the German newspapers in 1978.

Golden Wedding Anniversary

Sterbfritz (Kreis Schlüchtern). The married couple Richard Reinhard and wife, Kornelia, born Weismantel, were able to celebrate their Golden Anniversary on June 23 in Sterbfritz. Simultaneously, the jubilee began his 80th birthday.

Richard Reinhard established himself in Sterbfritz and was the first Catholic ever who took up his place of residence there. After difficult years at the beginning, the worse years of the Nazi-regime came upon him, his wife, and his children. One stood in opposition to the Great European Powers at that time, transmitted letters from Galen to others, secretly fed and cared for war prisoners, and hid Jews.

Disadvantages and imminent danger of death were the consequences. But partially because of luck and in part because of the support of amicably minded neighbors, the married couple, Reinhard, also survived these times. They are still to this day very vigorous and still maintain a dental practice. Eight children are congratulating them on this festivity, four of which live in America, along with their grandchildren. [Translated by Rosemarie R. Musso]

Some time ago, after speaking with my oldest sister in Germany on the telephone, she reflected on her memories about the evil plots that our family had to face during WWII. She recalled in 1945, before the war was finally over, the SS ordered the hanging of our whole family. The legal proceedings were initiated in February of 1945, and the hanging was to take place the end of March 1945. I can still remember my parents and siblings, with horror and disbelief, anticipating our family's hanging on a tree. Indeed, we surely would have been hung had it not been for the fact that the Americans had come into our village within only a few hours of our scheduled hanging. Thankfully, in the ensuing chaos, our lives were spared.

Actually, people in our village who feared for our lives ran toward the American troops, pleading for our lives and urging them to come to our home. Indeed, the Americans answered the plea of the people and did not delay one second. They rushed to our home, and saved our lives just hours before our hanging. Interestingly, when the American troops were close to our home, the would-be executioners ran away upon hearing of the approach of the American troops. Isn't that typical of the enemy? God is always on time, although I felt like He was really stretching it a little. What a miracle! This was a close call.

Not until now was I reminded about the story of Queen Esther, whom Mordecai raised as his own daughter. After Haman plotted to hang Mordecai and the rest of the Jews, Queen Esther pleaded with the king of Persia not only for her own life but for that of Mordecai and her people, the Jews. If you recall, Haman and his sons ended up on the very gallows that Haman had erected for Mordecai. What great vindication! Rather than Mordecai being hung, he was promoted and honored by the king. This event took place during the month of Purim, which precedes Passover. Like Mordecai, my father did not bow his knee to Hitler, his enemy, because my father had a fear of God, which was greater and stronger than the fear of man. This ultimately saved our lives. God honored him for that reason.

> **The Fear of God was greater and stronger than the Fear of Man**

At times, my father escaped the deadly consequences of reaching out to others simply by his great humor. Everyone knew Zahnarzt (dentist) Reinhard was endowed with humor.

Have You Ever Wondered If God Has a Sense of Humor?

I can tell you from personal experience that God loves humor. As a matter of fact, had God not endowed my father with great humor, we may not have survived; however, God brought him out of circumstances with such God-given humor that we were astounded. Let me tell you this little story:

You can imagine, with eight children and other family members residing in our home, there was a desperate demand for food. Needless to say, my father had to trust God to supply our food, for he had many mouths to feed during the war, including Jews and war prisoners. However, God had a plan. Time and time again, God continued to make provisions for us. Now, once again, God worked a miracle for our family. During these dreadful times when hunger was widespread, one of the farmers in our village gave my father a pig. Yes, here was a live pig in our home. But now what? After much effort and great skill, the pig was transported into our basement. Of course, my father decided to kill it secretly in our house in the basement, but how? He was desperate because we were on food rations, such as flour, sugar, meat, and potatoes. My father was determined not only to feed his huge family, but also to continue and secretly feed war prisoners.

In his distress, my father went to see his friend, the aforementioned veterinarian and told him about the pig in his basement. Thank God, the veterinarian agreed to come during the night to kill the pig as well as inspect the meat and make sure that everything was in order so that it was safe to eat. After literally putting his stamp of approval on the pig, he told my father that he needed to go to the store and purchase herbs and seasonings necessary to make sausages, which were to be smoked in a huge smoker in our attic. This was true luxury. Prior to his going to the store, this heavenly smell, at least it was to us, would have to be covered up. My father called another friend, his priest, and asked him to come to our house to shake his incense canister throughout the house—all three floors—so as to cover up the evident smell of the butchered pig which permeated the whole house before his patients would arrive for dental care.

Now, my father was ready to go to the store. Nervously, he went to the village store, and while my father was giving the owner of the store his list for these special and various seasonings, the owner was trying his best to give my father a warning by shaking his head while my father was ordering these special seasonings. Unfortunately, my father did not catch on when suddenly, a Nazi officer appeared on the scene and demanded my father to tell him why he was purchasing such seasoning.

Laughingly, my father replied, "Oh, I just killed a pig during the night."

The Nazi officer, shaking his finger at him, declared with a smile, "Oh, Reinhard, you and your jokes." Wow, is God good or what? He is—all the time.

People in the village were very well aware of my father's great humor which he used on his patients at times. For example, there was this young lady who came to see my father, and I will call her Mary. Mary was in pain. After my father examined her, he noticed a new wisdom tooth trying to make its way through her gum tissue. Excitedly, he looked at Mary, telling her, "Mary, you are going to have a little one." As my father recalled, Mary, suddenly with her eyes wide open, exclaimed, "Dr. Reinhard, how did you know?" She was under the impression that my father could tell she was pregnant. Was she ever surprised!

Another time, a farmer came to see my father whose teeth were really loose. Smilingly, he told him that he better go to the hardware store and purchase a big sack full of cement for his teeth. The patient was not sure whether my father was serious or just kidding. They had a good laugh.

Saved by Grace

Going back through the tunnel of my memories, I recall that my mother was very sick. My father sent my older sister to go to the village pharmacy to pick up my mother's prescription. As my sister was sharing her experience of meeting her teacher on that old cobblestone road on her way to the village pharmacy with me, grim memories of the brown uniforms our teachers had to wear in grammar school became very vivid to me.

During those times during the war, indoctrination in our schools was very real (nationalization of education). God was not to be mentioned. We were taught songs against the church and the pope as well as in praise of Hitler. If I should refuse to sing these songs at school, I would get in trouble, but if I sang them at home, I would be disciplined more severely. Either way, there was some sort of punishment. I chose to sing them at school.

The students were not allowed to greet the teachers with, "Good morning," but rather, we had to address them with, "Hail Hitler." Anywhere or at any time, whenever you ran into a teacher, it was for our benefit to great them with "Hail Hitler."

As my sister was rushing to the pharmacy, quite unexpectedly, she saw a teacher approaching her on the street. She was preparing to greet the teacher, although perplexed with the unexpected encounter. Now, with her thoughts racing in high gear at 100 miles an hour, she suddenly blurted out, "Holy Mary." Because of my mother's severe illness, she must have been praying for our mother; however, that was definitely the wrong greeting. Had it not been for God's grace, she would have suffered severe consequences, which she thankfully escaped that day.

I remember strolling through the meadows with a girlfriend close to our home while forced to suddenly hide and find some type of shelter from the incoming bombs and plunging bullets. Mostly, we found protection in the large wheat fields, which completely covered us. We never knew when the sirens would go off. We might be wandering through the woods in the early afternoon when suddenly we would be forced to quickly hide and find shelter from the air strikes. At that point, as fear crept in a little at a time, it soon would become my constant companion.

However, I knew that I could not give in to this tormenting fear but had to resist it on a daily basis. Eventually, I inwardly accepted fright and panic as an everyday occurrence and learned to simply exist from day to day. With time, it became easier to endure as this alarm and anxiety developed into what I assumed to be a "*normal*" lifestyle. Although I no longer have to operate under this fear, even to this day, I still have an eerie feeling when I hear airplanes flying over my home, especially if they fly very low or too close. Thank God, we survived despite my father's defiance toward Hitler by continuing to help POWs and Jews.

After the war, my father continued to practice as a dentist in our small village until he retired at the age of eighty-six, and my brother-in-law took over my father's practice. My dad passed away in 1991 at the age of ninety-seven. His legacy of love and commitment to help the Jews and POWs continues on in the lives of his family members, his children, and many others in our village he so selflessly helped. My father was a living testimony to the faithfulness of God's Word. He lived according to what is written in the Word of God, admonishing us to bless Israel as God promised Abraham in Genesis 12:3: "And I will bless them that bless thee, and curse them that curse thee; and in thee shall all families of the earth be blessed."

My father believed this, and so do I.

> **Battles are an opportunity to prove**
> **what you believe**

Retrospectively, I have had this opportunity to prove what I really believe on numerous occasions during my life, especially later in my life in my pursuit to study law.

Early in my life, I had to face battles. Hunger was never a stranger, but continued to be present and painful throughout my childhood. Moreover, because we were eight children and food was always scarce during war times, by the time I was six years old, I faced starvation along with my brothers and sisters. I was very lucky if I had a piece of dry bread to take to school, and that was considered lunch, and sometimes, I would even have some black coffee. As you are reading this incident, have you ever wondered whether or not you ever woke up in the morning not knowing if you would be able to have breakfast? Or maybe wake up at all—alive?

These feelings of anxiety and once again, fear, remained a constant companion, but eventually and with a sense of finality, I had to accept this plight and try to survive in spite of it. Had it not been for a wonderful nanny, Babette, who stayed with our family for over seventy years, we surely would have suffered even more because my mother had become severely ill.

Let me share her story with you. When Babette was very young, about six years of age, she was forced to sleep on straw in a farmer's kitchen. When my parents became aware of it, they took her in and welcomed her to the family. To me, she was a saint. Especially, during the war, she would walk to other villages across the railroad tracks just to get some potatoes or other kind of food from the farmers for our huge family. She took care of us until she died at the age of eighty-four. I still have warm and fond memories of Babette and still miss her.

She was honored when the mayor in our village presented her with a certificate for being in service for one family over seventy years and even received a special metal of service from the Pope in Rome. What an honor. She was absolutely great and always tried to fulfill our needs with her resourcefulness. Sometimes, though, there just was not enough; however, she truly made a difference.

The Pineapple Thief

Oftentimes, my uncle who lived in Chicago would send a care package to us, which was always received with much excitement. We were eagerly looking forward to such packages. Once a package arrived and was placed on the table in our dining room, my sisters and brothers seemingly turned into vultures hovering over the care package. On one of those occasions, because I was so little, I sneaked my way close to the package and, with lots of effort, I stuck my bony little arm into the package and discovered a shiny small can in the package. Hurriedly, I yanked it out of the package and quickly disappeared with my treasure and ran up into the attic.

Feverishly, I found something to partially pry the container open and with my little fingers and much effort fished out tiny little yellow pieces of fruit I had never seen. While eating everything out of the can, I thought I had died and gone to heaven. Nothing ever tasted so good. Unknown to me at that time, this was a can of pineapple. Worried about getting in trouble, I made my way to the garden, found a shovel and had a funeral for the can, burying it in our garden.

After this task was completed, I quickly went back to join the family in the dining room, hoping that the "pineapple thief" would not be exposed.

Needless to say, as a young child, I didn't understand the war. Fear and anxiety of the loud sirens and deafening noise of the bombs always, like a dark shadow, seemed to follow me everywhere. I didn't understand the loneliness I felt at times, and not being able to express to anyone how I felt, this emptiness in my soul would seem to mushroom. On numerous and countless times, I felt alone and scared. I simply did not understand why there was war. Recently, I found an acronym for war, and it read:

We

Are

Right

Just imagine, every party with a controversy shouting, "We are right." Of course, you know what happens when there is no compromise with either of the parties. Then, each one will prove through every means possible that they are right, even if they are wrong. Pride and narcissism takes over, and anyone who opposes such pride and control surely faces death. This is the theme of dictatorship. A dictator, like Hitler, says that only he is right and the rest of the country is wrong. He hungers and thirsts for power and control; there is no reasoning, and as a result, people suffer needlessly through atrocious, inhumane, and cruel acts by such dictators. That is war. How do you explain war to a child?

I didn't realize that war is the absence of love. Love was nonexistent, and as a result, I contributed this kind of existence to merely being a standard of living. Of course, my brothers and sisters and I did not experience the kind of nurture and love children need so desperately. Nevertheless, this was brought about by the necessity to survive in the face of a brutal and heartless dictatorship. We were victims of war and our surrounding circumstances. Personally, I did not know about love—that love was kind, love was to exalt someone else over yourself, and especially that someone showed his or her love toward another. I never heard the words but subconsciously longed to hear them from someone, *I love you* or *I care*. As a child, I was love starved. Love was completely foreign to me.

Everyone around us lived in fear and was at risk of facing hunger, even death. Being surrounded by death, fear, hunger, and distrust, this had become reality to me, day in and day out. Because I really didn't know any better to me, this became my way of life. Of course, I blamed God. Nevertheless, in the midst of chaos, God protected us no matter how bitter my thoughts toward Him had become. What a merciful God!

Among the many bombings, our house was just another random target, but God intervened. In 1944, the sirens went off with their thrilling sound. Then we heard the roaring noise piercing through the darkness of the night and the dreaded bomb was fast approaching our home. Much to our amazement, it passed over our house and exploded in the backyard.

Wow. Surprisingly, it only resulted in property damage—a shattered roof, windows blew out and shattered on the back of our home, and debris was scattered everywhere. What a miracle. Our lives were spared again. Amazingly, this event took place during the months of Purim and the Passover season. We were really scared. These were troublesome times, full of fear and anxiety.

My Baby Doll

At another time, while we were rushed into the basement during an air raid, I forgot my doll upstairs. Immediately, when I realized I left my doll, I tried to run back up the many stairs of our home to fetch my little doll. I certainly did not want her to die. I had to save her. However, I didn't get very far before I saw my father's strong arms reach for me as he angrily commanded me to sit down and not to move.

By a quick look in his dark, piercing eyes, I was quickly reminded to immediately obey, lest neither my doll nor I would survive if I disobeyed. You never argued with such a command by my father. There was silence for a little while which was suddenly broken by more air raids. We both survived.

Surviving the Bombings

Often, in the middle of the night, at the sound of the sirens, I could hear my older sister rushing to my bedroom and grab me like a bunny rabbit out of my bed to escape the screaming sirens threatening more bombs or shots from deep-flying pilots—the fighter planes. This happened usually during the night when the sky was dark and the moon gave a small glimpse of light. Shots were often fired through our windows, and this forced us to flee to our basement for temporary shelter. One of the bombs on that fateful night hit our neighbor's garage with our car in it, but at a time like this, who cares about a car? I recall the dark, black, threatening smoke and fire emanating from the neighbor's garage, but I also knew that our neighbors were with us safely in our basement. What a relief. God was with us in the midst of the fiery furnace.

Interestingly, when the huge dark clouds of tragedy are lurking in the atmosphere—when any kind of ambush is a lingering threat—we suddenly become aware of what is truly important in our lives. Do we call on God to help us? Absolutely. However, the best place to be in is to be prayed up in a dire and dreadful situation as this. However, God is a God of mercy regardless of our state.

During these dark times, there is a deep longing of survival and appreciation for life itself. Seemingly, material things become less and less important, while simply fighting to live becomes your most important priority. Shortly after that, another bomb hit the kindergarten behind our home. It was scary!

Oftentimes, I would crawl in a dark hole underneath the stairs leading into the main entrance of our home. The hole was large enough to keep garden tools in it; however, it became a security shelter and hiding place for me. I would crawl in there and stay in an almost fetal position for hours at times, hoping that no one would find me.

Although complete darkness filled that hole, allowing only a little daylight to creep in, I felt safe. I honestly didn't think that any bombs could reach my hiding place. Although being unaware of it, God was with me in that dark hole, and He is with us in our darkest, deepest times of despair. He is our hiding place. You, dear reader, may be in another type of dark hole in your life, full of darkness and despair, but trust me, God is there with you and will not let you perish.

Another Miracle.

I remember when my brother's high school was bombed, and my brother shared with us how his teacher died in his arms. How sad. Surprisingly, my brother was able to crawl out of the basement through the debris into safety and was even able to walk home for many miles. We thought surely he was dead. We were bewildered, yet truly excited when we saw him walking toward our home—with torn, bloody clothes and shaken, but alive. What divine protection!

Surprisingly, memories of my oldest sister's birthday are still freshly imprinted on my mind today. It was April 5, 1945. Bullets and grenades were being fired throughout our village. It was lunchtime. Suddenly, when no one expected it, a grenade passed straight and with great speed through our dining room window.

As usual, my sisters and brothers, my grandmother, dental assistants, as well as my parents and myself were having lunch in our dining room. While we were seated on each side of the table, a grenade destined to kill quickly, with deafening and ear-piercing sound, made its way through the middle of the table, barely passing my mother's ear as she sat now terrified at the end of the table. Amazingly, it landed in the light switch directly in the wall behind her. We were saved once again.

Needless to say, each of us immediately rushed into our basement for safety from the threatening and deadly grenades as well as to get relief from the loud sounds of the sirens. Once in the basement, a calm settled in without anyone speaking a word—a silent hush as if time was standing still as though contemplating the inevitable. We surely thought that we were going to die that day. Because it was my oldest sister's birthday, my mother had a small cake which she brought in the basement. To be able to even have a small piece of cake was, at that time, a miracle. Of course, that cake now had everyone's attention.

Immediately, knowing we were going to die soon anyway, we decided to eat the cake first. We were so excited about the cake that, for just a little while, we forgot about our fears of impending death and enjoyed the cake. We were not going to leave the cake for the Nazis. This brief moment of pleasure temporarily caused us to forget the imminent danger facing us. However, no matter what dangers were challenging and confronting us, my father never gave up on God, reminding us that God would get us through this and He did. My father trusted Him. God must have smiled on him at that moment, and our lives were spared again.

Sadly enough, as we were facing impending death on a regular basis, I never relied on God's help, but instead blamed God. Although unknown to me at that time, now, many years later, Psalm 23 became a reality in my life, which says that, "Yes, though I walk through the [deep, sunless] valley of the shadow of death, I will fear or dread no evil, for you are with me" (v. 4). This was obvious. During the fury of the war, we were eight children, and none of us was killed.

I finally realized that in order to face the Nazis, my father had to be tough and strict. I certainly had a change of heart toward my father. Much to my regret, it was not until later in my life that I understood that my father probably never learned how to express the love that was so deeply implanted in his soul: his love for God and His laws, and the love for his family.

God gave my father a supernatural compassion and love for war prisoners (POWs) and Jews, and that kind of love protected our whole family during the bitter years of WWII. It did not matter to my father who needed help, whether they were

Jews or POWs; a soldier, whether they were French, German, from Belgium, Holland, France, or East Germany; as well as refugees from Poland. My father reached out to all who were in desperate need and came for help.

The Refugee

Just recently I received an inspiring article from a gentleman, Karlheinz Kuhn, in Germany. He was desperately trying to find family members of my father. He performed an Internet search and was able to contact my older sister in Germany. After his conversation with my niece, he further pursued his search on the Internet and even discovered my daughter's ministry website.

Without further delay, he contacted my daughter and sent an email with an attached letter addressed to me about his mother's escape from Poland. Because the letter was in German, my daughter forwarded it to me, wondering about this mysterious letter. What a surprise after all these years. What was his reason for trying to reach my father's family members? Here is why. His story will touch your heart.

In 1943, his mother, Frau Ann Kahn, was forced to flee to Germany with her children from Oberschlesien, now Prudnik, Poland, near the southern border of Czechoslovakia. This long journey occurred during the bitter-cold winter and freezing temperatures. Along with her children, she traveled by train for fourteen days under the most horrendous and heartbreaking circumstances.

After this lengthy and painful travel, she was temporarily placed in southern Germany with people who were compelled to take her in as well as her children. This was mandatory. However, they only had to provide shelter for her and her children, but not any of the necessities, such as food or required furnishings in order to survive. She had to completely rely upon the neighbors' goodwill. Then, once more, after surviving under the most atrocious and horrific circumstances in Southern Germany, she and her children were transported to a small village in one of the surrounding villages of our family home, namely Oberzell. Frau Kahns's faith, courage, and resolve to survive and protect her children was miraculous.

Soon, among other hardships, she had to face another critical setback. Prior to her flight for safety, a dentist pulled all of her teeth due to a gum disease in exchange for her jewelry. However, when the dentist pulled her teeth, this dentist did not provide dentures for her; her only option was to survive toothless. How cruel!

While in her new and finally safe surroundings, she inquired about a dentist who would help her with her critical impediment. At that time, doctors and dentist were hard to find. Neighbors in her village recommended she go to see a dentist in Sterbfritz, our village, and he would probably help her.

Determined to find help, she walked alone for miles through the woods and finally arrived in our village and headed to my father's dental office. By then, an excitement arose deep within her soul. While in the dentist's waiting room filled with patients and standing room only, she was expectantly standing by the window, patiently waiting. Then, she saw an elderly man with white hair open the door and approach her. He smiled and then asked her, "Now, my dear lady, what is going on with you?" After he examined her, he simply told her, "You must have help."

Immediately, he took her to an examining room and made all the preparations necessary to make her dentures and scheduled her for another appointment a few weeks later. Upon her arrival at her next appointment, my father fitted her dentures. After she asked about the cost and my father being mindful that she was poor indeed, he simply told her to enjoy her new teeth and that all is well. After she returned to her home, someone asked her, *"Is that you or are you one of your youngest sisters?"* She was ecstatic. Such a compliment must have sounded like joyful music to her ears.

After many, many years, the son was eagerly trying to find one my father's family members to share his mother's story. Not knowing if my father was still alive, he set out to find a phone number for a family member. After making contact with my niece who happened to answer my oldest sister's phone, he explained the purpose of his call. After speaking with my niece in Germany, her instant reply was, *"Typical Opa"* (grandfather in German).

Because his mother shared her story with him, her son, Karlheinz Kuhn, who had learned of Dr. Reinhardt's benevolence to his mother prior to her death, wanted to thank him for his kindness to his mother, especially during such a difficult time. He wanted to thank my father and send a bouquet of flowers to him. He recalled that his mother wore these dentures with gratefulness and pride until the time of her death. After being informed that my father had passed away, he mentioned that now he could send a bouquet of flowers on behalf of his mother to my father in heaven.

PERSONAL NOTES

Hiding Emotions

Not surprisingly, even as children, we were drilled not to show any kind of emotions during these dreadful times and especially not to show the ever-present fear of the unknown dangers surrounding us. We had to be strong. Growing up, it seemed normal to me not to be able to cry (when in trouble) or express my feelings. Showing emotions was a "sin unto death" for us. Crying too much was showing weakness and resulted in being labeled as a wimp, whereas if laughing too loud, we would be marked as being hysterical. We had to heed the warning not to be too noisy.

Not being aware as a child of all the impending dangers lurking around us, we failed to realize that it was for our benefit and safety not to make a sound at certain times or confide in anyone. During these dreadful times, it most certainly could have been fatal to trust someone—another reason my father trained us in a severe manner not to show emotions or talk to anyone without permission. I never viewed this as an act of love by my father who was unwavering in his pursuit to protect us.

Did I understand this as a child? Absolutely not. Also, during the tough times of war, my father had a good reason to strictly forbid us to confide in or trust anyone. One would never know if your friend or once best friend was now capable of turning you in to the Nazis and ruthless servants of Hitler just to please the German Reich. Would it be a neighbor, a doctor, a business owner, or an old friend? What about your best friend? Truly, one would never know because of the mandated caution not to speak to anyone, and this was an awareness that was forever present. Hitler's power extended over all of the German people, caused much division and, of course, fear. We were not allowed to trust anyone. Consequently, the lack of communication with my father and even others caused me to feel great rejection and loneliness. I very quickly learned to keep my emotions hidden.

It soon became evident that the youth especially became brainwashed and served Hitler with such intensity that seemed to be far greater than any law to honor your mother and father. The Hitler youths no longer were independent thinkers but, under Hitler, became merely human puppets following Hitler to their ultimate demise. They were obedient to Hitler with such fervor that in their eagerness, quickly turned in their brothers and sisters, mother and father, or even their best friend to the Nazis without thinking twice. They followed the Fuehrer and complied blindly with every command. Of course, my father was very well aware of this.

This change was brought about by Hitler's call for nationalization of education to conform young people to think according to Hitler's standards as to how and what government wants students to think. What better way was there than for Hitler to indoctrinate the youth than through the national school system? Hitler had a subjective standard for schools. He wanted God out of government and schools—a godless society. Hitler's *number one* goal was to win the youths because then he would have control and bring them into conformity.

That is exactly what Abe Lincoln was talking about when he stated, *"The philosophy of the school room in one generation will be the philosophy of government in the next."*

Ultimately, growing up in a fearful, scary, and unsafe environment, only trying to survive, had made its mark on me. Eventually, I transformed all my negative hidden feelings about my natural father to my Heavenly Father as I started to compare them. I reasoned that my Heavenly Father would more than likely be just as strict and unapproachable, and I certainly could not trust him either. Furthermore, to me, He was doing all the terrible things, including the bombings, turmoil, fear, and hunger that had transpired or was apparent in Germany. For that reason, I therefore assumed that my father, God, and Hitler were all formed out of the same mold, and to be honest, I hated all three of them at that time. What an injustice!

As a result, my outer appearance as well as that of my siblings seemed to reflect that of living robots, but what inner turmoil there was. It was not until later in my life when I realized that the worst kind of starvation I suffered as a child was not so much physical, but it was the absence of love.

To me, this was a huge issue. Often, my mind would wonder back to certain events I really hated during the war, like having to go to school with ugly wooden shoes.

Wooden Shoes?

Yes, I remember the wooden shoes, which I only tolerated on my feet and longed to hide and discard while going to school. Times were tough during the war, and my parents could not afford leather shoes for eight children. Consequently, for a time, we had to wear horrible, hard, and inflexible pointed-toe wooden shoes. These, I am sure, came from Holland. No wonder I ended up with sores and scars on my feet as a result of wearing those ill-fitting shoes.

I will never forget the time when my parents were able to buy some "real" shoes for me. Oh, how much I admired my new shoes. I was elated. Was this a sign to me? Seemingly, with my new shoes, life got better little by little.

Although hope began to seep in slowly, at that time in my life, I had no idea what God had in store for me. I never realized life for me would drastically change. Even though it would be several years later, God still had an awesome plan for me.

God's Plan for Me.

After enduring the post-war era, finishing grammar school and finally graduating from high school, I began to help my father in his dental office. However, this was not to last. I was not able to stomach any of the oral surgeries he performed on his patients and once almost fainted as I was trying to hand him an instrument. That was the end of my dental career.

As time passed, I went to work for the United States Army in Fulda, the town where I went to high school that was not far from our home. I worked in the Special Services Department as a civilian. This afforded me the opportunity to improve my English. Sometimes I was able to engage in services with the transportation department. It was there when I met the man who was to be my future husband. He was stationed in Fulda and was a 1st Lieutenant in the Army and a commissary officer.

However, my father learned of my friendship with this officer. My father was not happy about this. It was not very long and without warning, my father showed up at my boss's office, a captain, just to let him know that, "My daughter just quit, and I am taking her home with me." Needless to say, I was stunned as I did not have any idea about this, and of course was absolutely dismayed.

After staying with my parents for some time, I then ventured out, with my parents' consent, to accept a position at the airport in Frankfurt, and I lived in a hotel close to my workplace. I was even able to walk to work. During that time, it was hard for me to develop any kind of close relationship with any of my friends but still enjoyed just spending time with them. Once again, I was trying to find some kind of personal fulfillment and love, but to no avail. Then, much to my surprise, the officer, Ross Musso, whom I had met in Fulda was transferred to Frankfurt, and we refreshed our friendship. Our relationship grew deeper as time went on.

However, this was to change soon. When it came to the attention of my father that the officer had been transferred to Frankfurt, he again did the unthinkable. He came to Frankfurt and quit my job for me once more. Now I was back to my parents' home. I was devastated. Soon after that, I pled with my father to allow the officer to come to our home to visit. After much pleading, my father finally gave in, finally approved of him, and gave his permission for us to get married. Wow, I was ecstatic. I got my wish.

However, was God trying to tell me something? I think so, but sometimes our own desires override those of the gentle whisper of the Holy Spirit. Often, when we are so determined to accomplish our goal or want something so badly, we do not weigh the consequences when we ought to be careful and heed God's warnings. He speaks through circumstances, and if we are not willing to heed counsel or see the handwriting on the wall or fail to see the red flags, God will allow us to travel on the path we chose. However, He loves us enough and is merciful, and He will eventually get us back on track. I was still unaware—or rather, destitute—of any knowledge or comprehension of God's Word. Little did I realize that our ways are not God's ways. Do you remember the song, "I Want It My Way"? God wanted my attention. However, that took some time.

At that point in time, little did I realize that I was to encounter the God of love later in my life—Love Himself— the one I hated for so many years. After coming to the United

States, God had a definite plan for my life, which was quite different from my own plans. How typical of Him!

In Germany, I was educated in a very strict Roman Catholic environment. The high school I attended was a convent which was operated by nuns who followed very rigid and strict rules and only allowed girls to be present at the school. The high school was located in Fulda and it required for me to take the train to school on a daily basis. Leaving our village early in the morning by 6:00 a.m. and returning by train about 4:00 o'clock in the afternoon was not an easy task.

Despite this religious upbringing, I did not really know the Lord or understand anything about having a personal relationship with Him during my high school years. Of course, I had a vast knowledge *about* God, but I did not have a personal relationship with Him. My studies about God were no different than any other history lessons. Actually, God did not mean any more to me historically than George Washington. Moreover, after graduating from high school, it became evident that there was no real transformation in the lifestyle I chose. Ironically, during the next few years, while I was running from God, looking for love in all the wrong places, God was making His plans for me.

How foolish I was to even think God doesn't love me. Seemingly forsaken, many times I would cry out to God, saying, "Oh God, there has to be at least one person in the world who might care about me." Sometimes, I would seek comfort in a downtown cathedral—just sitting there quietly, wondering if God really was there and heard me.

Then, finally, I did find that one person. I found out that He loved me unconditionally despite everything I have ever done. His name is Jesus. I was thirty-six years old when I finally surrendered my life to the Lord Jesus. What an impact this had on my life. Like Paul, I experienced an immediate transformation: from Saul to Paul. The "Saul" who had reigned in my heart died that day.

Immediately, I became serious about God and everything about Him. With my German background, it was easy for me to take God at His word. If God said it, I believed it. German people basically mean what they say, and frankly, they have a hard time with people who don't keep their word. After studying God's Word, I realized just how serious God is about speaking the truth. He can't lie. Can God expect any less from us? Absolutely not.

From the time I committed my life to the Lord, I expected people to be honest and speak the truth. Wow, was I ever set up for a rude awakening, and it didn't take very long! As I had etched in my memory the strictness of my father, who depicted absolute authority, I had painted a grim picture of God. Of course, I always viewed Him as an authority figure with a rod in his hand, and that included anyone else who had a place of authority in my life—for instance, a boss, a minister, pastor, or any other spiritual leader.

As a result of this stringent upbringing, I developed a healthy respect as well as obedience to any authority figure in my life, but this was always coupled with fear of authority. Regrettably though, I certainly had the wrong image of God, deeming God to be just as stern as my father, demanding absolute and immediate obedience at all times. My view of God had become very negative as I pictured Him as being without mercy and ready to judge me as soon as I made a blunder. I never credited God for being a God of love and mercy until after I had established a relationship with Him.

For the most part, I feared God; however, this was not a healthy fear of God, but an unjust feeling as well as an accusing negative attitude toward Him. In spite of my anger and a deeply embedded fear toward God, He showed me His love and His mercy. God knew exactly how I felt toward Him. At times, especially after I would tell God that I did not like Him because of my harsh childhood (accusing Him that He could have changed my circumstances), I felt that my ceiling was probably going to crash down on me, but He always forgave my condescending attitude toward Him and continued to love me. What a great God!

I was to learn to fight spiritual battles. Wow! At times I felt as if I were going through WWII again. Although the war was long over, I seemed to once again be in boot camp, which is an excellent training ground for discernment. I can tell you that true discernment comes not only through experience, but we must also understand the significance and fundamental truth to first rightly discern ourselves. Of necessity, this is the first requirement.

Only after we search our own soul and see our own short-comings or failures and judge ourselves will we have true discernment of others. Of course, above all, we need God's wisdom. Of course, wisdom comes from experience, and most of the time, it is very unpleasant. These experiences teach us to stand strong in the face of opposition. Try to recall your own disappointments.

PERSONAL NOTES

Do you remember how disappointing and devastating it can be when we finally realize that someone's words, especially those of a person in authority in our lives, were merely words masquerading as truth, hiding behind the mask of deception and meaninglessness—merely empty promises without any substance of truth?

Quite obviously, these types of impediments are designed to affect our trust not only toward that person (whoever it may be), but also toward our Heavenly Father because He represents truth. He is truth, and we expect the truth from anyone who represents Him. Therefore, when we become disheartened in these situations, it may catch us off balance until we are able, with God's help, to regroup. Sadly, as "baby" Christians, we are neither cognizant of these devices nor do we have the discernment to recognize that we are actually engaged in spiritual warfare.

Looking back, I thank God that He in His Wisdom knew that I would only grow spiritually by "way of Damascus." I gleaned much wisdom from God during those times and painfully and tearfully learned not to *lean on the arm of flesh* but to trust and rely on Him, and I would be safe.

Whether big or small, intentional or unintentional, I want to reiterate that these warfare strategies are designed by Satan to thwart our trust in God. It may just be a small, insignificant and minute offense, but it is those *little foxes that spoil the vine* (See Song of Solomon 2:15).

When People Wear Masks —
Mean What You Say!

I'll share a little example with you. It happened shortly after I arrived in the United States. My husband (now deceased) whom I met in Fulda took me to his church and introduced me to some of his friends and relatives. After the service, I was approached by a lady and several other people I had never met.

The lady was smiling as she was shaking my hand, blurting out with a shrill voice, "Oh, please come to see me," and immediately walked off.

Excitedly, I grabbed my husband and asked him to catch her as she had just *invited* me to her home but forgot to tell me the date and the time.

Laughingly, he replied, "Silly, that's just an expression. She probably didn't mean it."

I was devastated. Why would she say such a thing when she didn't mean it? Later, after I turned my life over to the Lord, He reminded me of this incident. In German culture, when one is asked to come see someone, it is taken literally, and future visits are immediately planned—date, time and place. However, much to my dismay, I quickly learned that her invitation was more of a polite (however insincere) gesture.

Today, I thank my father for the stringent and disciplined upbringing, although as a child I did not really appreciate it and wondered at times if my extremely stern father had not stepped into Hitler's footsteps. However, I realize now that my father had to be strict in the face of war and Hitler's opposition. Because of growing up during the war and utter turmoil, I learned early in my life that if you want to win, you can never give up, never quit, no matter how many trials and tests you are facing. If you want to fulfill your dream, you must never, never give up or look back on past failures or hardships, no matter what or how big or overwhelming your struggles may seem.

Anytime we experience some type of hindrances and obstacles, it will cause some type of pain. Pain is a signal that there is something wrong, something is out of order, but it helps you to know who you really are. Pain and opposition build character and integrity.

> **It takes courage to get back on track.**
> **Just don't quit and know God has your back.**

After the war, my father received the following letter from the Jewish Community Council in Frankfurt, thanking him for laying down his life for the Jewish people.

Below is the English translation:

Mr. Dentist Reinhard
6492 Sterbfritz
(Kr. Schlüchtern)

Dear Mr. Reinhard:

As we have learned, you were especially espoused to the cause of the war prisoners during the Nazi-regime.

We know exactly what grievous danger you were exposed to because of your helpfulness. There were only few people who were able to exhibit the kind of courage that was necessary and required for this.

The Board of Directors of the Jewish Council Frankfurt a. M. hereby takes the liberty to express our heartfelt thanks and wish you a happy and successful New Year and hope that the enclosed book will bring a little pleasure to you.

With Highest Regards,

JEWISH COMMUNITY COUNCIL
Director

[Translated by Rosemarie Reinhard Musso]

3

BACK TO SCHOOL

Immigrating to the United States

*A*fter entering the United States of America in New York in 1961, and arriving in the South, I eventually overcame my culture shock. My daughter, Barbara, was nine months old, and we spent some time in New York with relatives and my mother-in-law who came to meet us in New York. Thankfully, when the time approached to make our way to Birmingham, my mother-in-law flew back to Birmingham with my daughter in anticipation of our arrival in Birmingham, my new home.

I think it was during these formative years during WWII that I had made the resolve to come to the United States of America. To me, this was my Promised Land. After arriving in New York from Frankfurt, Germany, I could not wait to see the Statue of Liberty—America the Beautiful. Oh, this land was wonderful. I was in awe. There were so many things I saw that I had not even imagined in my wildest dreams. However, dreams change. Finally, we made it to what I perceived as the most beautiful site: the Statue of Liberty. I was determined to go see this historic site prior to our departure from New York.

How awesome! We spent a week in New York with relatives and then started our journey to Birmingham, Alabama.

During our trip to Birmingham, as I laid back in my seat in the little sports car we drove, I took in every detail of my new surroundings. Nonetheless, I couldn't help but muse about what I still called home, the beautiful country church in Germany where we were married, my parents, and especially my siblings. Doubts started creeping into my mind. Did I make a mistake? Did I truly just immigrate into a totally foreign country without perfecting the English language? Oh my goodness, what have I done? It was a feeling of excitement, and simultaneously I approached this situation with foreboding. Little did I know that I was in for a great surprise, and thank God, at that time, I had no idea what my future would hold. Once we arrived in Birmingham, my life was never to be the same.

It was not very long after my arrival in Birmingham, I knew that I had to make some serious new goals for my life. After pursuing new goals, I quickly learned that it would take some time for me to fulfill these goals and, once again, I had to face the task ahead of me to reach any of my targeted ambitions. By now, my oldest daughter, Barbara, was three years old, and by the time my second daughter, Christine, arrived, it became obvious to me that the time had come to pursue new dreams. My dreams started to crumble. However, because of my strict upbringing, I never showed my true feelings toward anyone. I had learned to hide and suppress my feelings and bury them deep in my soul, partly because of growing up during the war where death and uncertainties seemed to be a constant companion.

However, I was actually unaware of my hidden feelings until one day, a neighbor came to visit me and as we were talking, she questionably looked at me and voiced her opinion, saying, "Rosemarie, you are one of the coldest people I have ever met." Of course, I shared with her that as a child during the war, we were drilled not to show any kind of emotion, no matter what. It is not that I did not have any feelings; I had just learned not to show them.

Now, from the time I arrived in the United States, seven years had passed, and divorce seemed to be imminent. At that time, in Germany, you did not even mention divorce. After going home for a visit and letting my father know that I was filing for divorce, he could not believe it. A divorce? The sentiment about divorce was very negative. My father and others in our little village categorized the word *divorce* immediately after *murder*. After my visit in Germany, I decided to file for divorce.

Oh my goodness, what was I to do? I had to have a job. But how? To obtain employment only speaking high school British English, and moreover, without any kind of working experience in the United States seemed utterly ludicrous. What was I to do? As a starter, I had to learn business English. But how would I accomplish this? I set a goal.

First, I knew I had to go to business college to learn English if I wanted to find a good job in this country; more specifically, I wanted to be a legal secretary. Wow. Here were the mountains of doubt nagging me again, appearing very demonstrative and over-whelming, especially after nobody wanted to hire me because of my language handicap. Much to my surprise, I didn't even think about giving up. I knew I had to face these mountains head on. Finally, after twenty-plus interviews and exhausting all attempts for interviews, one attorney finally hired me, thus giving me a chance and an excellent start in the legal field. I will always be grateful to him. I loved it. What a challenge. I have worked for several large law firms since that time. I increased my legal skills, and had another dream to pursue my education—to become a paralegal.

Now it's time to move on again. For that, I needed an asso-ciate's degree in paralegal studies. Much to my surprise, with only a high school diploma from Germany, I passed the entrance exam at a state community college. I had to commune about one hundred miles from my home in Birmingham to school three nights a week while working during the day. This pro-cess lasted two years, at which time I received my associate's degree in paralegal studies, cum laude. Another miracle was that after being successful with obtaining an associate's degree, I set another goal—to obtain a bachelor's degree. After much prayer and receiving God's green light, I was elated.

By then, my two daughters, Barbara and Christine, had turned into beautiful young adults who had their own families, with an addition of four grandchildren. Of course, I had been the primary caretaker of my children after my divorce. At the time of the divorce, my oldest daughter was six, and my youngest daughter was only three years old. I tried to refuse all feelings of fear, which started to creep in on a daily basis. Again, my dreams were shattered. Nevertheless, as time passed, I also knew that I had no choice but to trust God. It was hard, but God helped me throughout my journey despite my faith taking a nose dive every now and then. Somehow, though, deep inside, I knew that no matter what, God would protect and guide me through life's darkest tunnel. He had done it before, and He will do it again.

Now it was time to move on once more. After I received my bachelor's degree, I realized and had a deep desire and a compassion in my soul to go to law school and become an attorney. I loved to study law. Now, I could pursue a new dream—law school.

By then, I had worked as a paralegal for a solo practitioner. Every time I had an opportunity to accompany my boss of fifteen years to court, I felt this warm sensation in my soul when entering a courtroom. To me, a court of law was awesome. God had planted this seed in my heart. Still, I knew that if I wanted to go to law school, I had to work during the day. Therefore, I chose to continue my education at night to pursue my bachelor's degree in order to enter law school. I enrolled at Faulkner University. Within one year and many, many midnight studies, I graduated with a bachelor's degree, cum laude, in Management of Human Resources. Despite the intense studies within this year, I loved the time I spent at Faulkner University. It was very rewarding.

Now, I was ready to go to law school, not knowing if I would make it through the first semester. Well, I did, and then I finally graduated from law school. I still had to face another mountain— two surgeries and passing the Bar. I could not allow my dream to die. It was a necessity for me to undergo a hip surgery in June. While in the hospital, I studied with tapes plugged into my ears for the Ethics exam. August came, and the Ethics exam was imminent. While still on crutches, I prayerfully decided to take the Ethics exam, followed by another hip surgery in September. I passed the ethics exam and was encouraged. At that time, I would have never believed that after gaining citizenship in 1977, raising a family, and attending hundreds of night school classes, I would make it to the top of my mountain and become a practicing attorney in the United States of America.

However, deep down inside, I knew that with God's help, I could do it. Then, finally, the dreaded day was at hand—the Bar exam. After getting stronger physically, I continued to study, study, study, and study some more. My studies began early in the morning until late, often after midnight. Relieved and exhausted, I finally survived both the Bar exam and the two surgeries, thus fulfilling my dream. I was on the top of my mountain, forgetting all the sacrifices and hardships I had to endure to reach the top and fulfill my dream.

I will always be grateful for the heritage with which my father equipped all of us children, teaching us to never bow down to obstacles, no matter how big or what the nature of the mountains are--whether these mountains represent a language handicap, lack of finances, children's trials, or never enough time. To reiterate, you can make it. Trials build character. My past, with all its trials and hardships, certainly helped me to overcome every challenge while I was trying to follow my dream to someday graduate from law school. My dream came true.

I have always known that God's hand was upon my father and our family and that I enjoyed His divine protection, and today I thank God for giving me the strength and the courage to fulfill my dream. I am thankful, too, that I can pass on my father's legacy of helping people. Was it easy? Absolutely not. However, without going through a valley, one would never reach a mountaintop. Climbing keeps your spirit, soul, and body healthy. It energizes your mind and, therefore, keeps your body going as well. A goal keeps your dream alive and encourages you to never give up until you reach your goal.

Ultimately, life's challenges will leave some wounds and some scars that have not had time to heal, but with God's help, we can rise above these battles if we don't nurture them. I vividly remember how discouraged I was when I found out that I did not pass the Bar the first time. However, it never occurred to me to quit. I had a goal, and I was determined to reach my goal. I just studied harder and harder.

It was during one of those years when I experienced a lot of difficulties and then additionally, my *only* boss, a sole practitioner, died, and I was left with no job and no money. This happened overnight, and it was to be a long time before I was able to get another job. However, it was during that period of time when God showed me that He was to be my provider, teaching me to trust Him and to forgive those who refused to help or even care. This was a hard task the Lord required of me—at least it was to me. I was crying out to God, "Oh God, I've got to have help. Either give me a breakthrough, a release from all this pain and anguish of my soul, or else just let me die. Help me or take me."

My world seemed to collapse. Does that sound familiar? The main reason for the despair and hopelessness I felt was due partly because of the pain and anguish I harbored in my soul and partly because of unforgiveness. I was in torment. Twenty-six years later and having learned how to have a relationship with God, especially learning to wait on Him, I simply asked the Lord for an answer and divine directions for my life. I was desperate. Then God answered.

It was December 6, 1987, about 4:30 a.m., when I was awakened from my sleep with a deep, deep voice (like a waterfall) resounding in my ear: "The Four Laws of Forgiveness, the Four Laws of Forgiveness, the Four Laws of Forgiveness," until finally, I realized God was speaking to me. I grabbed a pen and paper, and this message was birthed. That was twenty-nine years ago. I have never been able to communicate this until now. I have had to practice it. I had to become a doer of the Word and not just a hearer. God has now released me to share this message with the body of Christ. For me, it was a new beginning. I learned scriptural truth of how to overcome my misery. It seemed plain and simple: Forgive them. Now, don't get discouraged. Please read on.

PERSONAL NOTES

EXPRESSION OF GOD'S LOVE
His Last Wish

God showed me the importance of Jesus's statement, "Father, forgive them; for they know not what they do" (Luke 23:34). Have you ever seen or watched a person die or make a deathbed confession? Sometimes, for example, when someone is sentenced to death, the authorities give the person to be executed the opportunity to make one *last statement,* to say something he or she wishes to say right before one's execution.

Would you agree that knowing one has to die, the date is set and the time has come—the moment of execution—that if one should wish to make a statement of any nature, it would be the most important thing on their mind? It may be a statement, a plea that the death-row inmate, while suffering the consequences of his or her transgressions, would shout to others, admonishing them not to walk in their footsteps, or one might give some last-minute important detail, like root causes of what caused the problems and sin in their lives while adjuring others not to follow in their way of deception resulting in death.

It may simply be a good-bye or last words of affirmation, like "I love you." You know one's last statement to the world would be the truth and often an admonition that says, "It's too late for me, but you have time to change."

A few years ago in 1987, America and the whole world heard the plea of a woman in Texas who was executed in the electric chair. While in prison, she gave her heart to the Lord.

Although God had forgiven her sins, she still had to face the consequences of the murders she had committed. While incarcerated, she ministered to other inmates throughout the prison. She had made peace with God and man, and before her execution, she sent a message to the whole world: In essence, she was saying, "I am going to the electric chair, and I am willing to die for the crimes I have committed. It's too late for me, but it is not too late for you." *In Time Magazine,* she was portrayed as a "woman of faith, prayer and repentance." [3]

How much more significant do you think were the last words of Jesus, His dying declaration, *His last plea* to His Father while dying innocently on the cross for *our* sins: "Father, forgive them; for they know not what they do" (Luke 23:34).

Sometimes ignorance is bliss, but here Jesus acknowledged the ignorance of those who put Him on the cross. They were ignorant as to whom they crucified; they did not perceive that it was Jesus of Nazareth they nailed to that cross. Like so many today, they were blinded by a religious spirit. We do know better today. We do know it was Jesus Christ of Nazareth. We have God's written Word, the Bible. Therefore, as Christians, if we identify with Christ, then we must not ignore His example and the most important thing He did for us—His death on the cross for *our sins*—not His. The final expression of love by Jesus were his *last words: "Father, forgive them, for they know not what they do."* This was his last wish before His death.

PERSONAL NOTES

4

THE ENEMY'S DECEPTION

Satan's Lie

*W*hy is it so hard for us to follow His example of forgiveness? You know why? The enemy, our adversary, the devil, deceives us into thinking that we are justified by holding a grudge. Somebody hurts our feelings, or maybe we hurt theirs, and all of a sudden there is *war*. Suddenly a large gap, a gulf, has been created between two individuals. Satan tells us, "After all, they deserve what's coming to them. They *should* suffer.

Yes, because you had to endure pain, let them know what it feels like to hurt." Then he further admonishes us, "Get back at them, kill them, hang them, crucify them, and don't ever forgive them," and he goes on and on. "They caused you great anguish, they deserted you, they violated your confidence, they haven't forgiven you," and on top of that, "they utterly destroyed your life, so just annihilate them." You may say, "I have a right to be angry or upset." Really? Let's see.

Satan abides by his rules, which are always designed to deceive us because he wants to operate under his laws, which ultimately bring devastation and death. Not so with God's laws.

Certain laws of God are unchangeable laws, and I want to share four of those laws with you. Anytime you violate these laws, you voluntarily submit to Satan's laws and his authority over you. If you obey and stay under the authority of God's laws, you will prosper and stay under the umbrella of His protection.

Let me share these unchangeable laws with you as God shared them with me. If you will heed these laws, it will liberate you from your destructive or chaotic circumstances, whatever they may be: fear of rejection, self-rejection, resentment, anxiety, guilt, loss of a loved one, a husband or wife who left you, a child who rebels against you, fear of failure or loneliness, or guilt. Maybe someone slandered you or disappointed you; maybe friends or someone you trusted deceived or betrayed you; maybe someone took advantage of you, or maybe you are broke, maybe you just lost your job without cause, and as a result, you lost your home, or any other blow that the enemy would throw your way.

These laws will set you free so that you will no longer be bound by the torments of your heart and soul. You will have to make a choice as to which law you will follow: God's or Satan's.

The Lord gave me the four laws of forgiveness because we are not to rely on our opinions or feelings, but we must abide by His laws. For us to be able to walk in forgiveness, all four laws must operate. Forgiveness happens either to us (we are the recipient), or we have to forgive somebody else. One way or another, anytime there is forgiveness, regardless of whether we are the recipient or somebody else is, these four laws come into operation. Clearly, the Lord wants to set us free. Actually, it is so simple. It is merely a choice we make—an act of our will. We don't have to be bound up or shackled with an unforgiving spirit. You may ask, *but why or how would we be bound up, as if in chains, by this?*

Let's think about a person who has committed a crime. Suppose he or she is arrested and goes to prison. The police will arrest that person, put the suspect arms behind them, place them in handcuffs to restrict their movements, and haul them off to jail. There, the suspect will be confined for a certain period of time according to his or her charge of their crime. Now you are in jail—behind bars, unable to get out, at least for a time. That is what Satan does to you when you are not willing to forgive. He binds you up (as if with handcuffs), and you are becoming a prisoner of Satan where he is allowed to legally torment you at will. Now, Satan is not going to give you any warnings. He never does anything according to law. He just locks you up. Why?

Because of unforgiveness, we allow Satan to imprison us with chains and shackles of unforgiveness. We are bound up. Only we hold the key to get "out of jail." Unforgiveness is like a silent killer and is one of the major causes of unanswered prayer.

Jail is a stressful place, and until *you* decide to forgive, you won't get out. Doesn't unanswered prayer cause us stress?

Don't we often wonder why God doesn't answer our prayers? Not only do we wonder, but sometimes we even get mad, don't we? Have you ever been mad at God because you thought He did not hear you? Maybe you felt God didn't care? But of course, He cares. He loves you. That is why number one on our checklist to eliminate tension and frustration resulting from unanswered prayer is to check our communication line with the Father. Unforgiveness stops it up. Further, unforgiveness compounds our stress level.

In addition, if we allow stress to dominate our lives, it will cause medical problems. Unfortunately, though, God can't heal us because we absolutely refuse to forgive others for the wrong he or she may have done against us. Now, we find ourselves between a rock and a hard place. Our tension skyrockets if God will not meet our immediate demands. By now, we feel pressured because we did not get the answer to our prayers we so desperately needed, and additionally, we are sick. We really want God to heal us, but He can't. Not because God doesn't want to heal us, but he can't because He is bound by His own Word—His laws.

Unforgiveness binds God to His own laws. By holding on to unforgiveness, we are actually tying His hands. That is the worst kind of prison. Do you remember Jesus saying, "For if ye forgive men their trespasses, your Heavenly Father will also forgive you: But if ye forgive not men their trespasses, neither will your Father forgive your trespasses" (Matthew 6:14–15, *emphasis added*).

It goes on and on, and the snowball effect grows until *you* decide to put an end to it and forgive. *You* have to make the choice. God wants to set us free by being cognizant of the magnitude, the importance of forgiveness.

What does the word *forgiveness* mean? It is a function word to indicate the object or recipient of a perception, desire, or activity; it denotes, according to *The World Book Dictionary*,[4] a cause, a ground, or interest that you give for—or forgiving for. [5] It also means

- to give up the wish to punish or get even with;

- not have hard feelings at or toward; pardon; excuse;

- to give up all claims to; not demand payment for: *to forgive a debt (willingness to forgive)*;

- to give forgiveness (act of your will); pardon;

- a willingness to forgive;

- the remission of a debt, obligation, or penalty

In Greek, the word for "*to forgive*" is *charizomai* and means "to bestow a favor unconditionally and is used as the act of forgiveness."[5] This act of forgiveness can be human or divine, but whether human or divine, forgiveness must come by way of the cross. Let me explain:

We have to be obedient to God's word and His plan and purpose for our lives. Jesus bought our victory by His obedience to shed His blood on the cross. Why? To make us partakers with Him in this act of obedience.

It's not easy, but the Holy Spirit will help us to walk in obedience once we make the choice as an act of our will. Once we make that choice, there will be a shifting in the natural as well as in the spirit from unforgiveness to forgiveness. Jesus was obedient even when faced with death on the cross. He made the choice in the garden of Gethsemane: "Father, not my will, but yours be done" (Luke 22:42).

The Word says that "And almost all things are by the law purged with blood; and *without shedding of blood* is no remission [of sins]" (Hebrews 9:22, *emphasis added*).

I think it may help us to see what the cross itself stands for. As I was praying about this, the Lord directed me to study more about the cross. Listen to this:

According to the 1998 *Grolier Multimedia Encyclopedia* (TM) [6]:

> The cross is among the oldest and most universal symbols. In preliterate societies it often represented a conjunction of dualities. The horizontal arm was associated with the terrestrial [earthly], worldly, feminine, temporal, destructive, negative, passive, and death, while the vertical arm connoted the celestial [heavenly, divine], spiritual, masculine, eternal, creative, positive, active, and life.

Often symbolic of the four astrological elements of earth, water, fire, and air, a cross was also perceived as the cosmic axis from which radiated the spatial dimensions of height, length, width, and breadth, as well as the directions of north, east, south, and west (*explanations added*).

You see, Christ's death on the cross represented not only divine forgiveness but also human forgiveness:

Human Forgiveness

The *human act* of forgiveness is found in Ephesians 4:32, which says, "And become useful and helpful and kind to one another, tenderhearted, compassionate, understanding, loving hearted forgiving one another (readily and freely) as God in Christ forgave you." Human forgiveness is to be strictly analogous to divine "forgiveness."[7] Therefore, the human act is God enabling us by the power of the Holy Spirit to forgive each other (the horizontal part of the cross/terrestrial). It is conditional upon us forgiving others, and once we have met this condition, there is no limit as to Christ's forgiveness toward us. The conditions are *repentance and confession* (Matthew 18:15–17).[8]

Divine Forgiveness

When Jesus died on the cross, the veil was rent in two, from top to bottom (vertical/celestial—divine part of the cross), and because of that we were able to go directly into the Holy of Holies; it is through His blood and the removal of the veil when it was rent in two. It now gives us direct access to the Holy of Holies.

Another example when Jesus exercised *divine forgiveness* (of a debt) in Luke 7:40–43[9], when he spoke to a Pharisee by the name of Simon, who scorned Jesus because he let a woman (Mary Magdalene), who was a sinner, touch him in the Pharisee's house, and Jesus answered Simon, saying:

> "Simon, I have somewhat to say unto thee . . . There was a certain creditor which had two debtors: the one owed five hundred pence, and the other fifty. And when they had nothing to pay, he frankly (freely) forgave them both. Tell me therefore, which of them will love him most?"
>
> Simon answered and said, "I suppose that he, to whom he forgave most."
>
> And he said unto him, "Thou hast rightly judged" *(emphasis added)*.

Mary Magdalene had been forgiven much, and she in turn loved Jesus with the same depth of love that had reached out to her and forgave her. Her love was pure and unadulterated and was not tainted by the hypocrisy of the Pharisees, who wanted to see her punished for her sins. Why? The Pharisees were full of pride and were probably jealous of her relationship with Jesus.

They tried to hide their hate with their tremendous religious piousness. We must understand then that pride and hate are kin to religious self-righteousness and hypocrisy and by their nature are merciless—pride and hate will make no room for forgiveness. Hate and religion cry out for revenge, which is the work of the enemy, a real trap. There is no room in the Inn.

Therefore, forgiveness is terrestrial and celestial. However, we must meet one condition to be forgiven and thus enable us to be restored to a right relationship with the Father. What is that one condition? *We must forgive others their trespasses against us just as Christ has forgiven our trespasses against Him.*

Just as the veil to the Holy of Holies was rent in two, so likewise the veil of our flesh must be rent. Our flesh must of necessity be circumcised so that we will be able to forgive those who have trespassed against us. Only then will God be able to heal our emotions, hurts, wounds, and scars, as well as a broken spirit or a broken heart. The act of our forgiveness will not only bring healing to others, but it will boomerang and bring healing to our heart and soul as well. It is important to discern the sacrificial death of Jesus. We must realize that Jesus redeemed us not only from the penalty but also from the power of sin (earthly and heavenly).

Now, do you remember when Jesus cried out to the Father in the garden of Gethsemane while in great agony knowing His time to die had come? "Father, not my will, but [always] yours be done" (Luke 22:42). See, Jesus made a choice to do the Father's will. He is always showing us by His example what to do and *how* to accomplish what He asks us to do. In the same fashion, we must make a *choice* to forgive—that is to engage our will and make the decision to forgive. Sometimes, that is the hardest part: to will, to decide, to make that choice to forgive, but *we have to make a choice*.

Example of a Prayer for Forgiveness

Suppose you have to forgive someone who has really hurt and disappointed you, or maybe abandoned or mistreated you, unjustly rejected you, stolen from you, talked bad about you, slandered your name, or tried to assassinate your character. First renounce your right to, and let go of all anger, resentment, bitterness, revenge, or retaliation you feel in the Name of Jesus. You could pray something like this:

Father, I forgive *Johnny* or *Susie* as an act of my will, I now make the choice to forgive *Johnny* or *Susie* in obedience to your Word, not because I feel like it but as an act of my will. I now repent and renounce all of my anger, bitterness, unforgiveness, resentment, and feelings of retaliation against *Johnny* or *Susie* for (*here just tell the Lord what he/she has done to you*), and now, I hereby relinquish *Johnny* or *Susie* from my judgment and turn him or her over to your judgment. Then, pronounce a blessing upon *Johnny* or *Susie* according to Scripture. That really used to make me mad, but now I understand the importance of it. I will explain.

Jesus said, "Father, forgive them for they know not what they do." Maybe it would be easier or helpful to forgive once we realize that some people really don't know what they are doing. In the past, this was one of the hardest things for me to do—to forgive. I wanted to hold on to my feelings of anger, hurt, rejection, and self-rejection and wanted those who offended and hurt me to pay. Did I conveniently forget that Jesus died for my sins? That He put my sins in the sea of forgetfulness? That He washed me clean with His blood? Did I completely forget about that? Yes, of course.

When you are hurting, you don't want to think about Jesus. You want to justify yourself and have your payback time. That was especially true about my feelings toward Hitler. The farthest thing on my mind was to forgive him. Jesus understands that and will patiently wait until we are ready to forgive; however, he will bring you to a turning point of obedience to walk in forgiveness. Some of the bad memories about another person may still linger in your heart, but as you walk in forgiveness, the Lord will remove the hurt, the deep pain and the sting. You will be set free and these memories, although they may still be there, they will not affect or bother you anymore. Another important fact is to forgive yourself.

Did You Forgive Yourself?

Any time you ask God to forgive you for something you have done, no matter what it is, you know God will forgive you. The Word says that He is just and faithful to forgive. However, it is equally important and absolutely necessary that you forgive yourself. Jesus took care about any shame or guilt you feel, but once you repent of the wrong done, you are forgiven. Any bad feelings you have about what you have done after that is the work of the enemy to bring condemnation. Any guilt or shame are covered under the Blood of Jesus. Any guilt you may feel is certainly not from God.

Isaiah tells us that Jesus was despised and took the shame, so there is no need for you to take it, as well. You must accept that Jesus has done that for you already. What about things that happened in the past? The blood of Jesus has set you free and cleansed you from all guilt. You do not have to carry guilt once you have asked the Father to forgive you for your transgressions. Jesus took your guilt upon Himself on the cross. Forgive yourself.

Realize that God has forgiven you, including the guilt or shame you feel. It is finished. It is over. Bury any regrets, and do not waste any more of your precious time to dwell in the "sea of forgetfulness" where God so graciously put our sins and shortcomings once we ask Him for forgiveness.

However, here Satan will strike again. He will bring other Christians or believers of Jesus to randomly remind you of your past. Even then, keep walking in forgiveness. God will always vindicate you. I like what Corrie Ten Boom had to say about this, and I will paraphrase it. She reiterated that once we ask God for forgiveness, He forgives us all our sins and puts them into the sea of forgetfulness, but then a lot of well-meaning Christians will go deep-sea fishing in the sea of forgetfulness and bring all our sins all the way back up to the surface again and again. God really hates this ungodly attitude among His people. Was Christ's death then in vain? Absolutely not.

At that point, by making that *choice,* you will have won the victory over forgiveness because now Jesus can heal your emotions and remove any root of bitterness simply because you have given Him permission to do so. It is all by an act of our will. Then, you will be able to claim the victory that

Jesus already won on the cross: "But He was wounded for our transgressions" (*unforgiveness included*). Isaiah 53:3, verse 5, denotes that Jesus was a "Man of sorrows *and* pains, and acquainted with grief." We have to embrace the *Man of sorrows* in our lives rather than fight Him.

I know from my own experience, we don't like to identify with the "Man of sorrows and pains"; we don't like to walk with Him, but without identifying with Him, we will never really get to know Jesus. We have to die with Him so that we can be resurrected with Him—here on earth. What a wonderful and adventurous life we can have once we die to our flesh, ourselves, and make Jesus the Lord of our lives.

5

Jesus Cancels Our Debts

*J*esus, on the cross, canceled our "certificate of debt." By *His act of forgiveness,* He simultaneously disarmed the principalities and powers (*the rulers and authorities*) that were raged against us, and made a bold display and public example of them (Collosians 2:14–15, *emphasis mine*). Likewise, when we forgive others, there is a cancellation of debts and a disarming of the enemy. Here we can clearly see what Jesus accomplished on the cross. You see, Christ's forgiveness disarms the devil and leaves no open doors for the devil to torment us.

You see, Christ's forgiveness disarmed the devil in man's heavenward relationship (vertical-divine) with the Father; our pardon of others disarms the enemy in our earthly relationships (horizontal-human) toward one another.

What did Mary, the mother of Jesus, tell the disciples right before Jesus worked his first miracle in Canaan? Remember, she said, "Whatever He says to you, do it" (John 2:5). That's all we have to do—do what Jesus did. We are to be doers and not hearers only. Therefore, forgiveness is not only directed heavenward, from the Father toward us, but also horizontal, earthbound, from us toward others *from the north to the south and from the east to the west.* Didn't Jesus say, "If any person wills to come after me, let him deny himself [disown himself, forget, lose sight of himself and his own interests, refuse and give up himself] and take up his cross daily" (Luke 9:23)? Remember, the cross is both vertical and horizontal. When we pay the price and absorb the offense, we *release the power of God* and consequently bring not only healing to others but to our own soul as well.

Forgiveness is the very life of God. Here are some examples:

- *Look at Stephen.*

   As he collapsed under the magnitude of stones being hurled at him, like Jesus, falling on his knees, he cried out to the Father, "Lord, lay not this sin to their charge" (Acts 7:60). He forgave his adversaries. Stephen's forgiveness while he was being stoned caused the transformation from Saul to Paul, and it is designed to transform you and me.

- *Consider the reunion of Jacob and Esau.*

   Esau was a hardened man; yet when Jacob bowed down seven times to the ground in repentance, asking forgiveness from Esau, a flow of life directly emanating from the heart of God flooded Esau's embittered soul. An outpouring of grace went into Esau's heart, and the two brothers embraced and wept resulting in total healing. Esau had already forgiven Jacob, but when Jacob repented, through his act of repentance, forgiveness was released.

As they embraced and shed tears, all of their antagonistic past was wiped out. No grudges were carried over, no bad memories were dug up by either one of them, all guilt of past wrongs was abolished, and forgiveness flowed unconditionally. Then they were able to forget the past and thus enjoy tomorrow.

• *Remember Joseph?*

When he forgave his brothers, there was no bitterness, no revenge, and no angry last word that preceded his forgiveness. It was unconditional forgiveness, like Christ's. If we, like Joseph, forgive, we too *preserve life.* We restore our brothers and sisters to wholeness and bring great deliverance to them (Gen. 45:1–15).

• *What about Paul?*

Paul, at his first trial, said, "At my first trial no one acted in my defense [as my advocate] or took my part *or* [even] stood with me, but all forsook me. May it not be charged against them" (2 Tim. 4:16).

Forgiveness Is the Spirit of Heaven

By removing the hiding places of demonic activity, the deep inner scars, even the subconscious ugly memories from the depth of our soul, every wrong is made right, and every evil is redeemed for good. Thus, the power released in forgiveness is a mighty weapon of warfare. However, for us to be able to use this weapon, we must abide in Jesus. We have to recognize that Jesus is the Vine and we are the branches.

Don't the branches get nourishment from the Vine? Of course, we are nourished by drinking His blood and eating His flesh (John 6:53–56) and by staying in holy communion with Him. We have to consistently feed on and be nourished by the Word, and if we don't feed our spirit man with the Word, we become malnourished and weak. Consequently, if no nourishment is coming into us from the Vine, we eventually dry up and die—and Satan will have won.

We are admonished to be like Jesus. We sing, "I want to be like Jesus." When we take on the nature of Jesus and His character, we are abiding in Him, and then we will be like Him. How?

How do we abide in Jesus? Do what He did. Be obedient to His Word. We must obey.

Do what the Word says. Be a doer of the Word. Again, follow the advice of Mary, the mother of Jesus—do whatever He says. Jesus certainly was a doer in everything He accomplished while living on this earth, including his death.

Start sowing love and forgiveness, and you will reap forgiveness. That's abiding.

When we walk in love and obedience, we are abiding in *him*. When we, like Jesus, forgive in obedience to the Word, we will overcome the powers of darkness, stripping the enemy of his power over us. Walking in love and in forgiveness is one of the highest commandments. When we refuse to forgive, we come under the law. Where no love is, there must of necessity be the law, and the law is for the lawless. Remember:

> *Forgiveness is an act of our will. It is a choice. Jesus made this choice in the garden of Gethsemane.*

Jesus probably did not feel like praying like this, but He was obedient to the Father, praying, "Father, if you are willing, remove this cup from me: yet, not my will, but [always] yours be done" (Luke 22:42). He chose to go to the cross. He sowed the *seed of forgiveness* to mankind.

Forgiveness to Mankind

Forgiveness is very important because sin separates us from God, and without His forgiveness, we would live in total darkness and separation from God. *This was an act of unconditional love, and against love, there is no law. Love has no boundaries.*

- 1 Peter 4:8 — Above all things have intense and unfailing love for one another, for love covers a multitude of sins [forgives and disregards the offenses of others].

- Proverbs 10–12 — *Hatred stirs up contentions, but love covers all transgressions.*

- Romans 4:7 — Blessed are they whose iniquities are forgiven and whose sins are *covered (emphasis added)*.

How are they covered? With the *blood of Jesus*. The covering of our sins had to come through forgiveness, didn't it?

That was the supreme sacrifice, the atonement for our sins. From the very beginning of time, there always had to be a sacrifice in order to get into the Holy of Holies, to cover for our sins. Only love could do that forever. The Greek word *cover* in Romans 4:7 means "to cover up or over," meaning *atonement*.[10] "Blessed are they whose iniquities are forgiven and whose sins are covered." The Amplified version says, "Whose sins are covered up and completely buried" (Romans 4:7).

God's love forgave our sins through the atonement. His supreme sacrifice was His Son. You can only sow forgiveness through the law of love. The love of Jesus was poured out into the earth while He hung on the cross the moment He released His forgiveness: "Father, forgive them, for they know not what they do" (Luke 23:34).

To realize that people actually don't know what they are doing actually helped me a lot. Do you remember when God said that his people would perish for lack of knowledge? This also applies to taking matters into your own hands, by taking revenge yourself rather than extending forgiveness to others. You see, His love covered a great multitude of sins—the sins of the whole world. The power of love covered everything that we have ever done.

Matthew 26:28 says, "For this is my blood of the new testament which is shed (poured out) for many for the remission [forgiveness] of sins" *(emphasis added)*.

> ### *It covered and completely cleansed the filth and bloodstain of our souls.*

There are some striking truths we can glean from the word *forgive*. In Hebrew, *Sālah* means "to forgive."[11] This verb appears forty-six times in the Old Testament. The meaning "to forgive" is limited to biblical and rabbinic Hebrew; in Akkadian, the word means "to sprinkle," and in Aramaic and Syrian [the official language of the Persian Empire] it signifies "to pour out."[12] *Jesus, our Intercessor, poured Himself out.* It is also a type of intercession as seen in Isaiah 53:12: "Because He hath poured out His life unto death: and [He let Himself] be regarded as a criminal and be numbered with the transgressor, yet He bore and [took away] the sin of many and made intercession for the transgressors (the rebellious)."

Further, we will find the first biblical occurrence of intercession in Moses's prayer of intercession on behalf of the Israelites in Exodus 34:9: "If now, I have found favor and lovingkindness in Your sight, O Lord, let the Lord, I pray You, go in the midst of us, although it is a stiff-necked people; and pardon [*forgive*] our iniquity and our sin, and take us for Your inheritance" *(emphasis added)*.

When Jesus died for our sins on the cross and cried out, "Father, forgive them" (Luke 23:34), He was in intercession for us—*divine intercession*. Can you imagine the love of Jesus? He interceded for us even while being in agony and pain; this is beyond comprehension. He stood in the gap on our behalf without considering His own death on the cross. First John 3:8 reveals the purpose why Jesus came—to destroy the works of the devil. Isaiah told us that He went "Like a lamb that is led to the slaughter . . . So, He opened not his mouth" (Isaiah 53:7).

Now, even though we are forgiven by the Father, there are certain conditions we have to meet:

1. Repentance

2. Willingness to forgive others and, if necessary, to make restitution.

Yes, not only repentance but restitution is another very important factor of forgiveness. Have you ever been robbed or someone stole money or other personal property from you? What about slander or gossip that may have been a life-changing experience, causing serious harm? What about cheating? Did you not feel violated besides being angry?

While we indeed must forgive the person who harmed us, we should also hold them accountable, if feasible, to make restitution. That is, if it is at all possible. Whether we have been harmed or we have harmed someone else, restitution must be made the same as we expect restitution from others. Property has to be restored to its rightful owner or maybe financial restitution of making good any loss may be the right thing to do. Restitution simply means to *"to set things in order"* (Acts 3:21).

Oftentimes, it is not possible to make restitution or to repair the damage already done. That is especially true in a case of libel or slander. Sometimes, in such cases, just repent and know that God has forgiven you.

Restitution was required in the Old Testament. It is interesting to note that Leviticus 25:-28 teaches about redemption of land, and specifically in verse 29, it talks about the one year of redemption of a debt.

We only reap forgiveness if we sow forgiveness.

"And when you stand praying, forgive if ye have aught against any" (Mark 11:25). Don't we have a lot of aught against a lot of *anys* at times? *Webster's Dictionary*[13] defines *aught* as "anything whatsoever, all inclusive."

"But if you do not forgive others their trespasses [their reckless and willful sins, leaving them, letting them go, and giving up resentment], neither will your Father forgive you your trespasses" (Matthew 6:15). Think about this.

- How about the Lord's Prayer? "And forgive us our debts, as we also have forgiven (left, remitted and let go of the debts, and have given up resentment against) our debtors" (Matthew 6:12).

- "I, even I, am He who blots out and cancels your transgressions, for my own sake, and I will not remember your sins" (Isaiah 43:25).

- "Let the wicked forsake his way, and the unrighteous man his thoughts; and let him return to the Lord, and He will have love, pity and mercy for him; and to our God, for He will multiply to him *His* abundant pardon" (Isaiah 55:7, *emphasis added*).

- "And I will remember their deeds of unrighteousness no more" (Hebrews 8:12).

We should at all times ask the Father to make His promises real to us. It will not only make a difference now but in eternity as well.

Forgiveness Is a Spiritual Weapon!

Learn to use it. We cannot have victory over the enemy if unforgiveness is in our own heart. The choices we make depend on our attitude. You see, an *attitude is a condition of the heart*. Our natural attitudes must be replaced with the attitude of Christ. Only then can we win. Our attitude will be detected by our actions and/or our reactions. Remember, "As he [*a man*] thinketh in *his* heart, so is he" (Proverbs 23:7, *emphasis added*).

Our countenance will show our *real* personality; it will truly reveal the condition of our inner man and so will the fruits in our lives we display. Jesus said, "Ye shall know them (*his true disciples*) by their fruits" (Matthew 7:10, *emphasis added*).

Remember, forgiveness comes through the atoning blood of Jesus (Matthew 26:28), but cleansing comes by the Word of God.

Psalm 119:9 clears that up for us: "How shall a young man *cleanse his way?* By taking heed *and* keeping watch [on himself] according to your word [*conforming his life to it*]" (*emphasis mine*).

We need to understand that forgiveness and cleansing have different functions.

Jesus said to His disciples, "Now ye are clean through the word which I have spoken unto you" (John 15:3).

There is a certain *process* of forgiveness and cleansing:

(1) The blood for our sins

(2) The Word for our nature or character.

This is God's way of maturing us. For example, if we encounter unpleasant circumstances, we form an attitude. There is our attitude, but then there is also God's attitude, and there is a vast contrast between ours and *His*. Now we have a conflict. These are principles into which we have to mature.

Most of the time (if we are honest), we disagree with God on how to respond to certain circumstances. From past experiences, I know that how we react is most crucial. Somebody has to give in, and I can assure you, it is not going to be God.

Let the new nature (the Christ nature) become the *real you*. Ask Jesus, "Lord, show me. I am willing." You are submitting your will to His Word, His will, and His ways.

Again, Joseph is a primary example. After being sold into slavery by his brothers, he told them, "Ye thought evil against me, but God meant it for good." Joseph acknowledged the evil his brothers did, but he also acknowledged that God meant it for his good. Without reservation, Joseph acknowledged that God designs and engineers our circumstances for our good.

With this kind of understanding and knowledge of God's character, we will be set free from our fears when we face circumstances that upset or frighten us or cause us to panic. Joseph knew that God had a better plan and purpose for him in Egypt. He realized that it was God who made him ruler over Egypt, but it was via slavery, prison, and betrayal. God knew Joseph had a forgiving spirit. He always trusted God no matter what grim circumstances he faced. No matter who betrayed him, lied about him, and even when forgotten by the very person Joseph helped while in prison, his trust in God was so strong and pure that unforgiveness could not creep into his soul and defile him.

The Fear of God Kept Him Loyal

Joseph refused to yield to temptation when confronted by the beautiful wife of Potiphar, his boss. Joseph loved God so much that he chose to go to prison rather than sin against his God. The fear of God triumphed over the fear of man. He made up his mind. He was not going to give into temptation, whether sexual, pride, revenge, or any other temptation. Joseph kept his eyes on Jesus, which kept him in perfect peace, and ultimately, his faithfulness to God promoted him as ruler over Egypt. Did you notice, no matter what kind of promotions Joseph received, he never got caught up in pride? No, he remained humble.

Humility and holiness brought him the heavenly reward. God always honors obedience and submission to His Word.

Attitude Adjustment

So, what is our first step? An attitude adjustment? Do we need a checkup from the neck up and search our way of thinking, as well as our hearts? We have to learn and see God's pattern in our lives, look at the consequences of our behavior, and then see the end results. Get a long-range picture of your situation, not short range. Anytime we act out of a sudden impulse, we most likely will act and/or react with revenge, out of anger, hate, and jealousy or succumb to any other works of the flesh. Seeds of bitterness and resentment will always result in a harvest of bitterness, depression, and discontentment, and sometimes even death. When we allow ourselves to be bitter, we make ourselves a prisoner of our soul. Consequently, a root of bitterness will take root; eventually, this root will grow so big that most often, it will gradually choke the very life out of us. Thus spiritual death may follow.

This is the road of the carnal man, who is not spiritually minded. Have you ever met someone who will just "snap" your head off without a reason or reply with sarcasm to a very simple question? These displays of anger are symptoms of the root of bitterness constantly growing in an angry person. Acts 8:22 talks about the *thoughts of your heart*. Yes, the thoughts of your heart.

Typically, that's where it starts, doesn't it? It starts in our heart, and God's Word says, "So repent of this depravity *and wickedness* of yours and pray to the Lord that, if possible, this *contriving thought and purpose of your heart* may be removed and disregarded and forgiven you" (Acts 8:22, *emphasis added*).

When we start pondering in our hearts all the little things that bother us about someone else and we keep *meditating* upon these things, we are preparing a breeding ground for these thoughts which germinate and will gradually develop into actions. Thus, the enemy of our soul, the devil, has won the battle of our mind, which he specifically tailored to our particular circumstances. Remember, war never starts overnight. There has been enemy territory, which the devil has carefully prepared for his battle plan. His strategy to cause us to get into strife has been well planned, tailor-made. By feeding on hateful thoughts and dwelling on past failures and mistakes of the other person, we are giving Satan legal ground to strike. This is mentioned in Matthew 18:23–35, where Jesus told about the parable of the king who forgave a servant for a debt he owed, but the king *was moved with compassion* and forgave the servant.

However, this same servant who had just been forgiven for ten thousand talents ran into a fellow servant who owed him a hundred pence (approximately $20). Today, ten thousand talents would be worth about twelve million dollars, if one talent could be estimated to be worth about $1,200. However, with the fluctuation and inflation of precious metal prices, it could easily go up to a billion dollars.

His fellow servant asked him to have patience with him, but "he caught him by the throat and said, "Pay me what you owe." He would not forgive his fellow servant his debt. Now, when the king found out about this situation, the Bible says, "His lord was wroth, and delivered him to the *tormentors,* till he should pay all that was due unto him." Now, in verse 35, Jesus says, "So likewise *shall* my Heavenly Father do also unto you, if ye from your hearts forgive not every one his brother their trespasses."

Jesus always means what He says. Do you notice the word *shall?* It means "that is so, a done deal." Case closed. Can you afford not to forgive? Absolutely not. We have to take Jesus at His word. (The Word says that He cannot lie.) Certainly, we know that if we don't forgive, we will also be delivered to the tormentors, which are demon spirits, just like the wicked servant.

Have you ever wondered why some people always appear to be bitter, angry, or ready to fight for the most insignificant, minute issues? Why are they negative, critical, or judgmental? These people, for the most part, are being tormented by demon spirits because they choose to hang on to *their right* to be angry, *their right* to hold a grudge, and *they* choose not to forgive, thereby opening a door to a root of bitterness. When the anger, stubbornness, and refusal to forgive another persists or is prolonged, it will increase and spread like the dangerous, poisonous venom of a snake in your heart and soul, and soon the fruit of the "poisonous tree" within you will be evident in your countenance and behavior.

Yes, thoughts can defile us. When we keep meditating on the negative behavior of the one that has hurt us, it will produce and generate within us even more and more hate, anger, and bitterness. Hebrews 12:15 tells us, "Looking diligently [to look out for, to take heed, to oversee] lest any man fail of the grace of God; lest any *root of bitterness* springing up [germinate or grow] trouble *you,* and thereby many be defiled" (*emphasis mine*).

We must watch our thought life and guard our thoughts. A good antidote is Philippians 3:4, which encourages us to think on *good things—things that are of good report.* God knows what He is talking about. He already knew that when we think and focus on a "bad report" about someone, it will ultimately lead to strife, and "where envying and strife is, there is confusion and every evil work" (James 3:16). If you sow strife, that's what you will reap—confusion and every evil work.

If we do not operate in love and mercy, we certainly cannot draw love or mercy from the Father because His laws are unchangeable. To love one another is the second highest commandment of God, the first commandment being, *Thou shalt love the Lord thy God with all thy heart, and with all thy soul, and with all thy mind.* This is the first and great commandment. And the second *is* like unto it, *thou shalt love thy neighbor as thyself* (Matthew 22:37–39).

Sometimes, this is pretty hard to do, especially if you have a neighbor (that could be anyone you know, maybe a family member, a friend, an acquaintance, maybe someone at work, or maybe even a stranger) who is less than loveable -- one you want to avoid at any cost and stay far out of his or her way.

Romans 5:5 explains this love: "The love of God is shed abroad in our hearts by the Holy Ghost which is given unto us." This is a supernatural love through the help of the Holy Spirit. We can ask God to let *His love* flow through us because we cannot do this in our own strength. However, obedience is the key.

I recall Corrie Ten Boom sharing that "Forgiveness is an act of the will, and the will can function regardless of the temperature of the heart."

When we make a choice to obey, the Holy Spirit will empower us to carry out His commandments. Remember that "to obey is better than sacrifice" (1 Samuel 15:22). You absolutely must walk in obedience to God's Word. Jesus was obedient unto death, and the cross is part of our walk. He admonishes us to take up our cross on a daily basis (Luke 9:23). Love and forgiveness are a part of the cross. That is what the cross represents.

First, His love toward us and second, our love toward Him (vertical). Out of that celestial love relationship will be birthed the horizontal (terrestrial) love relationship among each other, whereby we can love and extend forgiveness toward one another. Without His love and forgiveness, there would be no cross.

Should we expect Jesus to be obedient to the Father unto death but we ourselves don't have to be obedient? A thousand times no. It takes faith to love and forgive; it takes faith to pick up our cross daily, but when we make the right choice, that is to be obedient *and do what the Word says,* we will be victorious in our faith walk. The Father always honors obedience. God is very adamant as to how we treat not only our brothers and sisters in the Lord but others as well. Do you exalt yourself above others? Do you respect your brothers and sisters both in the natural and spiritual—the people you work with or even those people standing in line in the grocery store? Do you let somebody else get ahead of you? Do you keep your word? We can *know* if we are truly walking in God's love or whether somebody else is by judging the fruit of a person. We can be fruit inspectors but not judges.

John 3:15–18 makes this relationship and attitude toward others very clear: "We know that we have passed from death unto life, because we love the brethren" *(emphasis added).* You are probably thinking, *Oh no, I can't love all these "brethren." Some of them are really unlovable. As a matter of fact, I can't stand to be around some of them.*

You are right. You can't love them on your own, but you can allow God to let His love flow through you, so you will be able to love the unlovable. I know this is hard, but once you make the choice to love and forgive, the Holy Spirit will enable you to reach out to that other person with His love. In my own life, it has happened quite often, especially at some of the places where I have worked or lived.

Sometimes there were people or a certain person I could not bear to even be in their presence, much less have to talk to them, and the thought of having to work with them was agonizing. At the same time, I was also keenly aware of their antagonistic feelings toward me. At first, I would ask the Lord to move them out of my way (as if He was really going to do that). After a while, by the time I was ready to move them out of the way myself, I found an alternative for God: "Well, Lord, if you are not going to move them out, move me." But guess what? He did neither. I had my own war going on. The characteristics of a person who refuses to forgive or to love are painfully described here:

> He that loveth not his brother abideth in death. Whosoever hateth his brother is a *murderer*, and ye know that no murderer hath eternal life abiding in him. Hereby perceive we the love of God, because he laid down his life for us: and we ought to lay down our lives for the brethren. But whoso hath this world's good, and seeth his brother have need, and shutteth up his bowels of compassion from him, how dwelleth the love of God in Him? My little children, let us *not love in word, neither in tongue; but in deed and in truth*. (1 John 3:14–18, *emphasis added*)

Obviously, to reiterate, God wants us to be *doers* of the Word and not only hearers.

Satan cannot force you to do his will, so he will sway or induce you to surrender to him. He is going to let you make the choice. Isn't he clever? Yes, the battlefield is our mind. That's where it begins. Maybe you are thinking about someone who lashed out at you or really hurt you in some way. Now you are meditating and logically dissecting every aspect of each and every offense, for example, how that person took advantage of you, talked about you, violated your confidence and even your friendship, and so forth. Moreover, you start strategizing and planning how you are going to show him or her or maybe show even several people your displeasure. You go on and on with your thought life and frantically wait to tell him or her off, letting them know what you are really thinking, such as that he or she has the morals of a scorpion, and the like until finally, you put your thoughts into action—you have a battle plan. Of course, then the other person strikes back, and before you know it, you think you are in the midst of Desert Storm.

Several years ago, there were several incidents where I was really angry about someone taking advantage of me, and I was complaining to the Lord about it. Repetitiously, I reminded God, saying things like, "Lord, you know how much I have helped that person. I was a friend. I laid down my life for that person, and now look, God, how that person paid me back." It was at a point in my life when my roots were literally taken up. I had to start all over again. I was crushed. Does that sound familiar? We keep reminding God of the wrong others have done to us, while we are so pious and see ourselves like innocent little lambs. Of course, sometimes we suffer from injustices done to us, but in due time, God will vindicate us from someone else's wrongdoing if our heart is right with Him. Then, we will experience the grace of God and whatever the devil meant for evil, God will turn it around for our good.

I am so glad God is merciful. Thank God He honored a request that I made of Him shortly after I got saved—that He would never allow me to get bitter, no matter what. God has honored that. Now He gently reminded me of that request and further reminded me of the beatitudes—that's how my *attitude* should be. I recalled the scriptures, though painfully, in Matthew 5:10–15:

> Blessed are they which are persecuted for righteousness' sake: for theirs is the kingdom of heaven.

> Blessed are ye, when men shall revile you, and *persecute* you, and shall say all manner of evil against you falsely, for my sake (emphasis mine).

> Rejoice, and be exceeding glad: for great is your reward in heaven: for so persecuted they the prophets which were before you.

Rejoice, Lord? You've got to be kidding. Finally, though, I realized that if I wanted God to bless me, I needed to change my attitude and get in line with the will and the Word of God. Not only that, but the Lord reminded me of His commandment (not a choice) in Matthew 5:44–45, Jesus said, "But I tell you, *Love your enemies,* bless them that curse you, do good to them that hate you, and pray for them which despitefully use you, and persecute you; That ye may be the children of your Father which is in heaven: for he maketh his sun to rise on the evil and on the good, and sendeth rain on the just and on the unjust" (*emphasis mine*).

I said, "Lord, this is truly a hard saying. Now I think I can relate to your disciples when they told you that." By now, I had to confess, "Lord, I don't have that kind of love in me, but I claim Romans 5:5 that the 'love of God be shed abroad in my heart.'" I asked the Lord to love my enemies through me by the power of the Holy Spirit and acknowledged that I was unable to love them with the kind of love I have. (By then, any love or mercy in me had taken a nose dive.)

Then God reminded me to change my "stinking thinking," my thought life. How? By looking closer at the word *forgive*. Love always operates in abundance; it is not stingy. Love affects the law of sowing and reaping: "He which soweth sparingly shall reap also sparingly; and he which soweth bountifully shall reap also bountifully" (2 Corinthians 9:6).

Sometimes, we encounter thoughts like, *Even if I forgive them, I am not going to forget.* That is not going to work. Keep reading and you will find that God will redeem your memories. It takes the love of Jesus in our heart to forgive, and that's why we have to abide in Him and depend on the power of the Holy Spirit to infuse this love into us and out through us toward the other person. That's what Romans 5:5 is talking about. Let's look at the word *forgiveness* and examine other meanings of this word that is causing us to stumble at times.

Forgiveness also means the "remission of the punishment due to sinful conduct or deliverance from the penalty of sin: the complete removal of the *cause of the offense based on the sacrifice of Christ.*"[14] In the Old Testament, the atoning sacrifice and forgiveness are often associated and closely related to each other.

Leviticus 4:14-19 sets out the ceremonial sin offerings through animal sacrifice in the Old Testament. In the New Testament, Jesus was the sin offering Himself. The biblical view of sin, however, does not depend wholly upon the concept of law; it appeals to the holy character of God Jehovah—Holy God:

> When the sin, which they have sinned against it, is known, then the congregation shall offer a *young bullock for the sin*, and bring him before the tabernacle or the congregation. And the elders of the congregation shall lay their hands upon the head of the bullock before the Lord; and the bullock shall be killed before the Lord.

> And the priest that is anointed shall bring the bullock's blood to the tabernacle of the congregation. And the priest shall dip his finger in *some* of the blood, and sprinkle it seven times before the Lord, even before the veil. And he shall put *some* of the blood upon the horns of the altar which *is* before the Lord that is in the tabernacle of the congregation, and shall pour out all the blood at the bottom of the altar of the burnt offering, which is at the door of the tabernacle

of the congregation. And he shall take all his fat from him, and burn it upon the altar.

And he shall do with the bullock as he did with the bullock for a *sin offering,* so shall he do with this: and the priest shall make an atonement for them, and it shall be forgiven them. (Leviticus 4:20, *emphasis added*)

It is very important that we understand what forgiveness means. Why and how? We can find the answer in John 3:16: "*For* God so loved the world that He *gave* His only begotten son" (*emphasis mine*).

The word *for* has a big significance because it denotes the cause or reason, the root, *why* God *gave* His only Son. The reason is simply this: "That we would not perish, but have everlasting life" (John 3:16). The word *forgive* itself gives the answer. Let's look at it more closely:

The Father *for [gave]* us our sins when He *gave* (his son) *for* all the sins and atrocities we have ever committed, inclusive of all the punishment we so deserve. Therefore, forgiveness is part of giving because you are giving of yourself; you are giving something up for a cause, that is, your own right to hurt, to be wounded, to be bitter, to be disappointed, or even to take up an offense and revenge you so desperately desire. It is the *total and complete* removal *of the* cause *of the offense.* That's what He *gave for.*

God *gave* Jesus, the sacrificial lamb, as atonement *for* our sins; *only* for *that reason he gave* His only son, for you and for me.

116

Let's take a closer look at the meaning of the word *"for"* in the *Black's Law Dictionary:*

- *For* within the legal sense means:
  In behalf of, in place of, in lieu of, instead of, representing, as being which, or equivalent to which, and sometimes imports agency . . . Duration, when put in connection with time. . . .

- In consideration for, as an equivalent for, in exchange for, in place of; as where property is agreed to be given for other property or *for* services **(as in an exchange)** *(emphasis added)*.

- By reason of; with respect to; *for benefit of;* for *use* of; in consideration of. The cause, motive or occasion of an act, state or condition . . . because of . . . on account of . . . in consequence of . . . by means of or growing out of. It also *connotes the end with reference to which anything is, acts, serves, or is done* (*emphasis mine*). [15]

Jesus's act was a legal act to cancel, void, or rescind Satan's contract and authority, which Adam, through his disobedience, gave Satan over us. While Jesus was dying, He proclaimed, "It is finished." The battle came to an end. It was finished. The *seed* was buried, died, and rose to new life in three days for you and for me. Now, let's take a closer look and summarize the four laws of forgiveness.

PERSONAL NOTES

6

THE FOUR LAWS OF FORGIVENESS

I. THE LAW OF SOWING AND REAPING

Strategies for the Battle Plan

*T*he law of sowing and reaping is an unchangeable law. Let's start with John 3:16: "*For* God so loved the world, that he *gave* His only begotten son . . . *(emphasis added)*. What was God doing at that point? God was *sowing the seed of love, His Son—the Word, Jesus.* He, the Father, gave out of love. He sowed love because He wanted to reap a full harvest. Genesis 3:15 says, "And I will put enmity between thee and the woman, and between thy *seed* and her *seed;* it shall bruise thy head, and thou shalt bruise his heel" *(emphasis added)*.

He *sowed* the *seed* of love (the seed of the woman) and planted that seed with a promise: to bruise the enemy's heel. The seed grew up and became flesh, and the *seed,* Jesus, became the Lord of the harvest. When God sowed the *seed* of the woman, he was actually initiating *the law of sowing and reaping,* thereby opening the door for redemption. God planted the *seed, Himself,* into the woman. He always sows first.

As you know, love is the highest law of God. God is love; by desiring a large harvest of love, God is desirous of reproducing

Himself in us and through us. As you know, any kind of land has to be cultivated in order to produce a ripe, good harvest. You know, in Jeremiah. 4:3, the Word speaks of breaking up our fallow ground [our hearts]; the hearts of stone have to be replaced with hearts of flesh, and the process of cultivation is usually somewhat painful. God's best for us is to be like *Him,* to be like Jesus. For that to take place, we have to be broken in our soulish realm so that the spirit man can rule and reign in our hearts.

The process of pruning, breaking, and cultivating takes time, but God's timing is always perfect. When God gave His Word, Jesus, He had a due season for reaping from what He had sown. Always, according to the law of nature, there is a certain time and season for sowing and reaping, just like the seasons of the year—spring, summer, fall, and winter. There is nothing we can change about that; I don't think you could plant a rose garden in the middle of winter, in the snow. It's the wrong season.

There has to be the right season for sowing. The harvest depends on what you sow. If you put plum seeds into the ground, and you really want to grow an apple tree, don't expect apples to grow on that tree; if you want apples, then you must, out of necessity, plant *apple seeds.* If you want peaches, plant *peach seeds.* Every tree bears fruit after its own kind. We need to be like these spiritual trees who bear fruit after their own kind. What kind of fruit is this? You need to ask yourself, "Do other people see your fruit and, as a result, grow closer to the Lord?" A person who bears really good fruit will always exhibit love, be helpful, long-suffering, persevere, will not spout insults against you, is filled with fruit exhibiting love; and is always ready to extend a helpful hand.

These are truly the fruits of real disciples of Christ. They are always ready to minister to the needs of others, often neglecting their own needs but wanting to spread the love and mercy of God everywhere. These are disciples of the Lord who will not pick up an offense for even the tiniest, minute offenses. They will be quick to forgive and overlook an offense—these are fruit trees with luscious, healthy, and delicious fruit. You just love to be around people like that.

Now realize that whatever you are sowing, you will also reap when the harvest comes. Undoubtedly, you have heard many times that expression, "You reap what you sow." Actually, this is talking about the law of sowing and reaping. Many of you have probably used the expression, "What goes around comes around;" this is essentially a spiritual law of sowing and reaping. Also be aware of the fact that you can't plant a seed today and expect your harvest tomorrow. You can't plant apple seeds today, and tomorrow morning go outside and expect to see an apple tree. We know that is foolish in the natural, but God's truth is parallel; thus, it is just as foolish in the spiritual realm. There is a *due season*.

The Bible speaks of a *due season* and admonishes us "not to get weary in well doing . . . we will reap . . . if we faint not" (Galatians 6:9). God's grace and mercy brings us through these hard places. Whenever we think we are going to faint or when we think we can't go another step, God helps us not to faint and to fight the good fight of faith. Any time we go through those dark places in our lives, God is working things out *within* us rather than doing anything *for* us. The purpose is to cause us to be strong, trust Him, and develop character and integrity. Is it easy? Absolutely not. But if you can't trust God, who else could you trust? No one. He is the only one you can trust, even in the midst of the storm. I would add that you should trust Him in the midst of the storm because if you don't, failure or disaster will be the result. I can speak from personal experience about this truth.

Now, remember, one of the Greek root words for *forgiveness* is *aphiemi* and means "to send forth, to send away," and denotes, besides other meanings, *"to remit, to forgive."* When the Father *gave His Word and sent forth* His Son, His Seed of Love, the Father's expectation was to produce a great harvest out of that Seed:

> For as the rain and snow come down from the heavens, and return not here again, but water the earth and make it bring forth and sprout, that it may give *seed to the sower* and bread to the eater *so shall my Word be that goes forth out of my mouth;* it shall *not* return to Me void [without producing any effect, useless] but it shall *accomplish* that which I please and purpose and it shall prosper in the thing for which I sent it. (Isaiah 55:10–11, *emphasis added*).

It is the same with God's Word. It is harvest time (Joel 3:13). These seeds of forgiveness are ready to spring up. God compares

His Word to a seed. The Word shall not return to God void. Just like the water is poured into the earth, the *words* of Jesus, "Father, forgive them" (Luke 23:34), they watered **the earth as a seed of His forgiveness. Now, the harvest is ripe and makes it bring forth and bud or blossom** so that, as Isaiah stated, "it may give seed to the sower, and bread to the eater." That's the way it is, and that's the way it's going to be. We cannot change God's unchangeable laws. You reap what you sow. That's it.

God has an appointed time in our lives to bear fruit (not to be fruitcakes but to bear fruit). He wants to build character in us (not have a bunch of characters). He wants us to bear fruit. "And he shall be like a tree planted by the rivers of water, that bringeth forth his fruit in his season" (Psalm 1:3, *emphasis added*). God declared that we shall bring forth fruit in *our season*.

Fruit is produce. Have you not gone to the supermarket or the farmer's market and bought fresh produce? Now, I am sure that you would not buy produce that is not ripe, but you pick out the fruit that looks the best, don't you? Notice that luscious fruit was a seed first, and then like all produce, the seed had to grow until it was ripe. You already know it takes time for fruit to grow and ripen, right? *The Word (the seed) is Jesus.* Jesus was conceived in Mary's womb, and after nine months, He was born; He became flesh. God had a plan. He had a certain timing for Jesus to be born and to die on the cross, so that prophecy could be fulfilled. *Jesus is the incorruptible seed* who is inside of us, waiting for us to mature in Him and to bear fruit. There was a due season for His birth as well as his death.

Jesus, the Word in the Flesh, was aware of His assignment to be crucified while being tortured and ridiculed by the Roman soldiers. He knew beforehand that this was going to happen. Yet, knowing He was going to die, "[H]e went like a lamb to the slaughter; [H]e opened not His mouth" (Isaiah 53:7). He was obedient to the Father.

When He cried out, "*Father, forgive them,* for they know not what they do" (Luke 23:34), Jesus sowed His intercession for us to receive forgiveness from the Father. Jesus had already forgiven us. Now, we are reaping the harvest and all the benefits from this sacrificial act, and there are many benefits flowing out of forgiveness. It not only restored our fellowship with the Father, but the same blood that was shed for our forgiveness will cleanse us and bring reconciliation to our relationship with each other (Colossians 1:20–21).

When we ask our Father to forgive us, and as we humble ourselves before the Father, while releasing forgiveness to others, we are sowing seeds and giving power to His Word simply by acting in obedience to it.

There is power in forgiveness that will disarm the enemy.

And you, being dead in your sins and the uncircumcision of your flesh, hath he quickened together with him, having forgiven you all trespasses; Blotting out the handwriting of ordinances that was against us, which was contrary to us, and took it out of the way, nailing it to his cross; And having spoiled principalities and powers he made a show of them openly, triumphing over them in it. (Colossians 2:15)

When Jesus cried, "Father, forgive them," every demonic principality and power which had infiltrated man's relationship with God was disarmed. When He spoke, "Father, forgive them; for they know not what they do" (Luke 23:34), hell's gates unlocked, tombs opened, the veil into the Holy Place was rent and heaven itself opened, all because of His forgiveness. Even many dead arose (Matthew 27:51–53).

God's *power* was released through Christ's intercession. That was the Father's supreme sacrifice—His own son. Jesus could have cried, "Father, consume them. Let the earth swallow them up, hang them, crucify them. I don't deserve this. I certainly have a right to be angry. Look how they humiliated me. Send a legion of angels and just wipe them out," but He didn't.

He gave up bitterness, resentment, hurt, bruises, rejection, horrific pain, and all the other horrible and dastardly atrocities directed against Him by the Roman soldiers. Why? Because of His love and obedience to the Father. He is love, He sowed love, and now He wants to reap our love. *Jesus is the Lord of the Harvest* (Matthew 9:37–38). What do we learn about intercession from Jesus? That's love on its knees.

Jesus needs laborers. These are the people who are willing to sow of themselves into someone else's life out of their own need, people who follow the Lord Jesus by example and deed.

These are true disciples—people who are willing to forgive and stand ready to fight the good fight of faith. Jesus said that the harvest is indeed plentiful, but the laborers are few, and actually commanded us to pray the Lord of the Harvest to force out and thrust laborers into His harvest. God needs laborers, not whiners—people who walk in love and forgiveness and, thus, are ready to labor in His kingdom.

Remember Gideon? If you read about Gideon, you will note that God sent all the weaklings home. He could not use them during war. Each and every day we are engaged in spiritual warfare. That's why it is so important for us to stay strong and resist our enemy with strength and not weakness. It takes a strong person to sow the seed of love. God cannot use weaklings in His army. We should go to work as *sowers with seeds of love*.

This is one truth that has helped me in the past, and it is this—a truly spiritual person lives above injustices and wrongs done to him or her by men or women because he or she knows that God engineers and orchestrates all our circumstances. He understands God's testing, His patterns of blessings and/or chastisements in our lives. What is God purpose? Ultimately, God is interested in the fruits of the Holy Spirit being birthed and brought to visible fruition in our lives: character, integrity, and maturity.

If your answer to God is *yes,* you will choose to walk in love by the power of the Holy Spirit, and you will have to pass the endurance, patience, perseverance, and hardships tests. You won't faint. You will walk in victory without a baggage full of wounds and hurts; you will cast them on Jesus.

Then, and only then, will God be able to use you and trust you with His power. The end result? God can accomplish everything through you and give you everything He had purposed for you from the beginning, before the foundation of the world. His plan and purpose for your life will be fulfilled. With God's power and with God's help, we can walk in His love.

Let me tell you a little story the Lord gave me on a trip to a client's house while working on a case as guardian ad litem. The place was in a very remote area several hours from Birmingham. After driving for several hours, I ended up in an area where I saw nothing but trees. I knew I was in the country. I called my client and asked for further directions. I could hardly believe his reply:

"When you drive just a little further, you will see a goat, then call me, and I will meet you there."

"A goat?" I exclaimed.

The answer was the same: "Yes, a goat."

After continuing down the country road with huge trees hovering over both sides of my car, I was looking for a goat. Finally, behind a fence on the left side of the road, much to my astonishment, I actually saw the goat and a sheep. Surprised to see both, I called him, and as promised, he met me down the dirt road, and I was able to follow him to his house.

Upon leaving, he asked me, "Do you know what kind of a goat that is?" Of course, when he saw the blank stare on my face, he volunteered to tell me that this was a *fainting goat.*

"What in the world is a fainting goat?" I asked.

He explained to me that fainting goats are easily startled. Should you approach them and make any kind of noise, they get startled, fall to the ground, and actually faint. On my trip back to Birmingham, I couldn't help but to meditate and think about this fainting goat. While thinking about that, the Lord showed me, like he usually does in a parable, that we humans are much like these fainting goats. I wondered about this and had to admit that when we hear noises in life, what is our approach? The Word tells us that our enemy comes like a roaring lion seeking to devour us. How? He is looking for us to open the door. Most often, when we hear the *noises* in our daily lives, we want to faint and give up. Maybe not immediately, but the enemy uses these tactics to divert our attention to him rather than keep our eyes on God.

What are some of those noises?

- Discouragement or depression, resulting from feelings of hopelessness and the inability to cope with insurmountable stress or pain, physically or mentally, and other extremely loud noises.

- Disappointments and fear of feeling inadequate are noises which are designed to drown you in despair and finally do the unthinkable which would cause you to just give up. That is where the enemy will win. Do not pay attention to these noises—they are designed to destroy your spirit, soul and your mind. Keep the mind of Christ, and *never give up*. Don't listen to these enemies of your soul, and you will be the *winner*.

- Fear of failure, trauma from death of a loved one, shame, or any other type of fears with their paralyzing effect will attempt to stop you from reaching your dream and being successful.

- Some of these noises affect us because of unforgiveness.

As in my case, one of the biggest noises I faced was the torment of fear during WWII: fear of hunger, loneliness, rejection, feeling of inadequacy, not measuring up to others, resulting in fear of man, disappointments, and especially fear of death during WWII. Later in my life, I still had to face the enemy of fear when it started to creep in once more in other areas of my life, especially after my divorce in a foreign country. I continued to struggle with fear—fear of the unknown, fear of not being able to take care of my two children, fear of the future, and on and on.

Then again, another type of fear struck when I went back to school in the United States. The enemy once again showed its ugly head prior to and during exams not only at the community college in Gadsden or Faulkner University, but especially before and during the Bar exam. Yes, to me these fears were very real; they were the kind of fears which appeared to be paralyzing.

I had to face them and overcome them. Little did I realize that a lot of these fears were partly triggered by the fears I had experienced during WWII of self-doubt, the fear of not accomplishing my goals, as well as a hardened heart because of unforgiveness. Of course, most students experience these typical anxieties prior to dreaded exams; nevertheless, we still have to overcome these fears and face them head on. I am not talking about just a normal fear prior to exams, but the *paralyzing kind* of fears.

Once I acknowledged and saw these fears as noises of unforgiveness, which were designed to distract me and partly because of my lingering distrust in God (again, my faith had taken a nose dive), I had to learn to completely trust Him. Once I made up my mind to trust Him, my fears gradually vanished. This did not happen overnight, but it happened gradually. As my trust in God became stronger, I began to have more peace.

How many times do we humans get startled and just faint? Life in general will throw noises at you no matter how old or how young you are, whether you are male or female. Those noises which we encounter at times are also designed as opposition, which we will face in almost every situation during our lifetime. Nevertheless, they are only noises. However, we can't be like the fainting goats and just faint. We ought to realize that any time we experience opposition, it will cause some type of pain. What lessons do we learn from obstacles and hindrances? I realized that pain is a signal that there is something wrong, something is out of order, but it helps to know who you really are.

Are you a winner or a quitter? Do you really want to win, or will you just give up and quit? Will you give in to your fears or overcome them?

It makes a difference which you will choose. If you make the quality decision to win, God will reward you with success; however, on the contrary, should you decide to just throw in the towel and quit, then the enemy of your soul will be the winner. That is precisely the reason why God will instill in you the *fear of God* and not with man and with God's help, you can overcome this fear of man. If he will do it for me, he will do it for you. My father was a great example for me in this regard to oppose and never allow the fear of man destroy the future God had planned for our family and for me. Don't let him win. You be the winner, the victor.

Pain and opposition will build character and integrity. It will let us know of what kind of stuff we are made. It takes courage to get back on track, and oftentimes it takes an act of forgiveness.

The moral of the story is that we should not be fainting goats. God needs overcomers. So don't be a fainting goat. Keep going.

God Hates Religion

We need to understand that God hates religion. Sometimes we meet people who say all the right things, but their actions are contrary to the Word of God. Make no mistake about it, God says from such detach yourself; He separated the darkness from the light. God admonishes, even demands, that we not have anything to do with adulterers, liars, and so forth. Whenever we do anything contrary to God's Word, we are not walking in love. We can't say we love God and at the same time violate His Word, His commandments.

We can't escape the fact that God wants doers of the Word and not only hearers. He needs disciples. We can't live in fornication, adultery, lying, or cheating, or maybe not keep your Word (personal or business) and then ask God to bless us. When God says something, he takes it very seriously. The same applies when we promise someone else to do something but do not keep our Word; then God says we are liars. That will not work because our *seeds* of rebellion will bring a harvest of heartaches and pain.

According to Hosea 8:7, if we sow to the wind, we will reap a whirlwind. Remember Hitler? He sowed hate and destruction, and Germany reaped the Holocaust. Why was he able to do that? As mentioned previously, no one, not even the church, spoke up. No one saw the warning signs or red flags, or if they did, they just ignored them until it was too late. I cannot emphasize enough that the silence of the church and the people in Germany made it easy for Hitler to win. Today, we must speak up, draw a line in the sand, and say, "Enough is enough."

Our forefathers paved our way on Christian principles, and we should take a stand to defend them as they are the cornerstone of our Christian foundation. If we don't, we will reap destruction.

As the church, it is necessary that we take action or suffer the consequences. One of Hitler's first official act after coming to power was to get God out of government, the schools, and even the church. If we do not honor God, He will not honor us. As a precondition, we have to sow that which is good and right, and we will reap a bountiful harvest—every time, all the time. It is an unchangeable law.

Forgive Hitler?

God had been dealing with me that I must forgive everyone from all of the grievous hurts I had experienced during WWII, including Hitler. Astonished, I asked God if I had to forgive Hitler as I still harbored a lot of hate in my heart toward him. To me, he was one that should never be forgiven. How I was astounded when I heard a strong reply, *"Of course you do."*

Forgive Hitler? No way, Lord. Lord, you've got to be kidding. Forgive Hitler? Forgive the Nazis? You know what this monster did, don't you? Suddenly I realized what the disciples meant when they told Jesus, "Lord, *this is a hard saying; who can listen to it?*" (John 6:60–69). I was really able to relate. In verse 60, many of the disciples quit. They refused to follow Jesus and murmured. That is exactly what I was doing. Now, it was time to exercise my will. Do I forgive, or do I continue to murmur and hate and ultimately quit following Jesus?

You know who always wins though. I finally ended up even forgiving Hitler. This was a hard decision to make. I not only forgave Hitler himself, but all the Nazis as well. I truly even repented of Germany's abominations and horrific acts toward the Jewish people during the Holocaust. Of course, as you know now, I had to make that choice. Wouldn't you like for Jesus to say to you after it's all over, "Well *done,* my good and faithful servant"?

Hitler never understood the law of sowing and reaping. His idol was only himself—power. He was a typical narcissist. He only sowed seeds of poison, corruption, and fear. Remember, his theme was to be brutal and to destroy everything and everyone who opposed him. To forgive Hitler was one of the hardest things I ever had to do, knowing what devastation he brought to Germany, the millions of innocent people he killed and slaughtered, and the thousands and thousands of lives he devastated, including my family.

God impressed upon me over and over that by my forgiving him was *not* for Hitler's benefit but only for my benefit. Once I grasped this truth, I was at least able to forgive him as an act of my will, in total and complete disregard of any feelings I had toward him. God had to do the rest. However, I made that choice in obedience to His will—even while gritting my teeth.

Now it was up to God to complete the healing process. What was the harvest of Hitler's horrible seeds? The Holocaust. At this point, let me admonish you to sow, sow, sow love, and *you* will reap a harvest of love and forgiveness from others. To further understand forgiveness, let's look at the next law.

PERSONAL NOTES

II. LAW OF BINDING AND LOOSING

Holding Someone in Bondage

Whatsoever you shall bind on earth shall be bound in heaven, and whatsoever you shall loose on earth shall be loosed in heaven. (Matthew 18:18)

Judge not, and ye shall not be judged, condemn not, and ye shall not be condemned, forgive, and ye shall be forgiven *(released)* (Luke 6:37, *emphasis added*).

The Greek word for forgiveness in Luke 6:37 is *apo/uo* and has the following meaning: *apo*—"from" and *uo*—"to release, to let loose from," and is translated, "Forgive," meaning, "you shall be released." You may ask, released from what?

When you forgive, you are actually setting the other person free as a quasi-judicial act, you dismiss him or her, and by doing that you are giving God the liberty to deal with that person.

Look at Matthew 18:21–35, which reads, "Then the Lord of that servant was moved with compassion, and *loosed* him and forgave him his debt" (released him) *(emphasis added)*.

He *loosed* or *released* him. Likewise, when you release the person from your judgment, you turn him or her over directly to the Father. By the act of relinquishing your right to deal with the other person, you release your right to revenge or to bring judgment yourself, your right to pick up the offense—your right

to be angry or your right to retaliate. In other words, you are setting the other person free or untying them from your restraint.

Now you are allowing the Father, by the Spirit of God, to
deal with him or her. We can do no less than what Jesus did.
He released us from our sins, and by doing that, He released
us from the bondage of sin and the penalty of sin; thus, we can
now go straight to the Father through the blood of Jesus. We
have immediate access to the Father's throne.

Jesus released the thief on the cross and then, while dying,
cried out, "Father, forgive them" (Luke 23:34).

The work of Jesus was finished. The veil was rent. As you
recall, the veil in the temple separated the Ark of the Covenant
from the people who were shut out by the veil. Only once a
year, on the Day of Atonement, the high priest was able to enter
beyond the veil to appear in the presence of God for the people.
A priest had to go in on the people's behalf.

The veil was the only way to get into God's presence, and
as stated, man was shut off from direct communication with
God. That's why John the Baptist cried, "Behold the Lamb of
God who takes away the sin of the world" (John 1:29). God
had a Passover Lamb. Interestingly, it was the fourteenth day of
Nisan, the day to slay the Lamb that the Lamb was slain. There
He hung, the covenant sacrifice, the veil of *His* flesh ripped in
two for you and for me so that we no longer will be separated
from the Father.

> **There is no other way to enter into God's presence except through the rent veil of His flesh. Through His death, He paved the way into the Holy of Holies.**

Now it is up to us to say to God, "By faith and as an act of my will, I choose to walk in love and forgive. I choose to die daily." Make a declaration: "Death to my old way of life, death to my independent life, death to my rights, death to taking up offenses, and death to self." This is true repentance.

Have you ever had a dead person snap back at you or get offended? No, of course not. We have to discipline our flesh and our soul to overcome in the area of our will our emotions and self-centeredness. If we don't stop focusing on self, we will end up in self-pity, resulting in all kinds of pity parties (I know, I have been the guest of honor at my pity parties lots of times). That is certainly not pleasing to God. It hinders us from being all God wants us to be.

What a shame that Satan can deceive us by playing mind games, causing us to exalt ourselves above others. The Scriptures admonish us to edify one another and to exalt our brothers and sisters above ourselves.

Being offended will surely choke the Word of God in you, eventually resulting in spiritual death. Therefore, being offended and staying offended, my friend, is deadly. This is why Jesus said, "For whosoever will save his life shall lose it: and whosoever will *lose his life* for my sake shall find it" (Matthew 16:25, *emphasis added*). Jesus forgave. He died so that we could live.

Yes, there He hung: *the Way, the Truth and the Life:*

- the *Way* we should walk,

- the *Truth* we should live, and

- the *Life* by which we should live.

PERSONAL NOTES

III. THE LAW OF PERPETUITY

Eternal Laws

Webster's Dictionary defines *perpetuity* as "endless: time" or "the quality or state of being perpetual."[16] It deals with time. Eternal laws are unlimited, endless.

God is not bound by time. His laws do not change; they are timeless, eternal. By and through His laws, God's nature is always revealed. His attributes and His laws always reveal His character, and God wants His nature and character revealed through us, not only on Planet Earth but in eternity. The more of His nature we take on now, the more He can trust us with His power and upholding our responsibilities in the future on this earth and, finally, eternally.

Everything we do affects us in the present *and* in eternity.

When we forgive, we are operating in His laws, and thus, we reflect or are reflectors of His laws, His nature, His attributes, and His character. When Jesus forgave us on the cross, it was not only for our benefit while we live on this earth, but it was eternal so that when we leave this earth, we will be in Jesus's presence and ultimately rule and reign with Him. God always has a long-range or long-term plan.

He is never shortsighted, nor has He tunnel vision. You see, that is why the seeds of forgiveness you are sowing now are eternal because you are operating in and enforcing God's eternal laws. Your harvest, therefore, will not only be in the now but will also reach into eternity. Remember the horizontal part of the cross, which is earthly or terrestrial, and the vertical part, which is celestial—eternal? Please meditate on the following scriptures:

> For thou, Lord, art good, and ready to forgive, and plenteous in mercy unto *all* them that call upon thee (Psalm 86:5, *emphasis added*).

> Moreover if thy brother shall trespass against thee, go and tell him his fault between thee and him alone: if he shall hear thee, thou hast gained thy brother. But if he will not hear thee, then take with thee one or two more, that in the mouth of two or three witnesses every word may be established. And if he shall neglect to hear them, tell *it* unto the church: but if he neglect to hear the church, let him be unto thee as a heathen man and a publican. (Matthew 18:15–17, *emphasis added*)

> Then came Peter to him, and said, "Lord, how oft shall my brother sin against me, and I forgive him? Till seven times?" Jesus saith unto him, "I say not unto thee, until seven times: but, until seventy times seven." (Matthew 18:21-22)

How many times did Jesus say you have to forgive? Seventy times seven. As you can see, there are no limits, no borders— east, west, north, or south—to Christ's laws of forgiveness, but certain conditions have to be met. His laws when enforced upon the earth will immediately be effective on earth, but the value and consequences of the very act of forgiveness is eternal as well. You see, if you do not forgive, you cannot *ever* be forgiven by the Father. You may be thinking that you don't want to forgive or you just can't, or you may say to yourself, "Well, my father, mother, sister, brother, or maybe a friend or coworker surely meet their daily quota to be forgiven. Seventy times seven is a lot of forgiving." Nevertheless, I am sure that we have met our quota at times with others. For true forgiveness to take place, there has to be

(1) Repentance

(2) Confession (1 John 1:9)

And if he trespass against thee, rebuke him, and if he repent, forgive him. And if he trespass against thee seven times in a day, and seven times in a day turn again to thee, saying I repent, thou shalt forgive him (Luke 17:3, 4).

And be ye kind one to another, tenderhearted, forgiving one another, even as God for Christ's sake hath forgiven you (Ephesians 4:32).

"A certain lender of money had two debtors: one owed him 500 *damaris*, and the other 50. See, when they had no means of paying, he freely forgave them both. Now which of them will love him more?" Simon answered and told the Lord, "I suppose that he, to whom he forgave most." And he said unto him, "Thou hast rightly judged" (Luke 7:40–43).

The more forgiveness we have experienced, either from God or man, the greater our love should be toward him. He set the precedent. There is a legal term, "quid pro quo," which means "this for that." What we give, we receive. Quid pro quo.

This for that. Therefore, in order to receive forgiveness, we must likewise *freely forgive*.

An important lesson for us in understanding the law of sowing and reaping is a teaching I heard from Mike Murdock: *you will always be remembered by either the problems you solve or the problems you create,* and like Mother Teresa always proclaimed and I paraphrase, that a kind word may be very short, but the effects of kindness will be forever.

PERSONAL NOTES

_____

_____

_____

_____

_____

_____

_____

_____

_____

_____

_____

_____

_____

_____

_____

_____

_____

_____

_____

IV. *LAW OF FAITH AND RIGHTEOUSNESS*
Making Choices

For us to understand the Law of Righteousness and how it works, we need to understand the origin of righteousness. Romans 3:22–28 speaks of God's righteousness:

Even the righteousness [from the Greek word *dikaiosune,* meaning "equity" of character or act; or specifically, "justification: righteousness."] of God which is by faith of Jesus Christ unto all and upon all them that believe: for there is no difference.

Romans 3:22–28:

For all have sinned, and come short of the glory of God; Being justified freely by his grace through the redemption that is in Christ Jesus: Whom God hath set forth *to be* a propitiation through faith in his blood, to declare his righteousness for the remission of sins that are past, through the forbearance of God;

To declare, I say, at this time his righteousness: that he might be just, and the justifier of him which believeth in Jesus. Where *is* boasting then? It is excluded. By what law? Of works? Nay: but by the law of faith. Therefore we conclude that a man is justified by faith without the deeds of the law *(emphasis added)*.

As you can see, *righteousness* works by the law of faith, and faith works by love. Hence, righteousness is produced through love. This is a principle by which the Holy Spirit acts as an imparter of life. Therefore, we have found deliverance from the law of sin by the shedding of blood (Hebrews 9:20). His laws operate by righteousness, through faith, because He is Righteousness Himself. These laws could not operate in any other way except to produce the life-giving Spirit through us, which is manifested within us by the fruits of the Holy Spirit. These are the laws of the Spirit of Life in Christ Jesus, motivated by the anointing and power of the Holy Spirit.

Therefore, we are not under the law of sin and death but subject to the obedience of Christ, who delivered us from the powers of darkness and translated us into the kingdom of His dear Son (Colossians 1:13). Remember, these laws are unchangeable laws. Romans 8:2 says that, "For the law of the Spirit of life in Christ Jesus hath made me free from the law of sin and death. Where is boasting then? It is excluded. By what law? Of works? Nay: but by the law of faith."

Now, because of Him, we are able to do what is pleasing in His sight, to be righteous in Him, by His laws. What is the motivator to be righteous in Him? The motivator is love. Love will produce fruits of righteousness. Other people who are starving for love will be drawn to us; their souls and spirits will be able to freely eat of our fruit (love, kindness, gentleness, patience, perseverance, long-suffering, and so forth) and be satisfied. People are craving for that part of the fruit in His disciples that forgive and forget, that do not hold grudges; that part of the fruit of the Holy Spirit that will do what is right no matter what.

That is the law of faith through our righteousness in Him. We accept His righteousness by faith because we are righteous in Him, not in ourselves. In Christ, we can excel in everything we do, whatever our task is, and no matter what comes against us because we can walk by faith as we mature into righteousness.

The more we mature in Christ, the easier our walk of forgiving others will be. When maturity comes, God's wisdom in everything we do will be prevalent in our lives. I saw a poster in a grocery store several years ago that read:

> *Right is right—even if nobody does it.*
> *Wrong is wrong—even if everybody does it.*

Faith operates by love. We have to exercise faith to believe for healing for those who are sick. James 5:15–16 talks about the prayer of faith, saying, "And if he have committed sins, they shall be forgiven him." God makes provisions for us when we yield to Him and walk in His love. Jesus is a perfect example. He always walked with compassion. He provided both food for the body and food for the soul—a smile, a hug, and compassion when someone was sick. He was there. You may want to read these scriptures:

- Healing: 2 Chronicles 30:18–20—the Lord pardoned and healed them. Verse 19 tells us that we have to *set our heart to seek and yearn for God.*

- Colossians 1:14—Redemption through Christ's death. Also: not a penalty.

- Galatians 5:22–23—Against these, the fruits of the Spirit, there is no law.

We have to be led by the Spirit.

- Romans 3:27—the Law of Faith

- Romans 7:23—the Law of mind (warring with flesh).

Imprint this in your heart and soul: the law of the spirit of life has set us free from the law of sin and death.

We are no longer subject to the law of sin and death; however, you have to make the choice under which law you want to serve.

After I came to America, it took some time for me to see these truths. Did I forgive my father? God? The people who refused to help us? The people who betrayed us during the war and almost caused us to be killed? Regrettably, it was not for a long time. I did not want to forgive and was comfortable in my own war zone. Not until I decided to live for the Lord, Jesus, I walked in darkness and unforgiveness. After that, the Holy Spirit started to convict me and put people in my life who were able to teach me about forgiveness and simply *letting go* of all those tormenting feelings.

At that time, it was hard for me to relate to walking in love and forgive. I was forced to make a decision—forgive or not to forgive. God demanded it. By faith and setting aside my feelings, I simply forgave each and every one as an act of my will. It was simply an act of obedience. Indeed, I needed God's help with this because of a lot of antagonistic feelings that were rooted deep down in my soul, my subconscious. Finally, after surrendering my struggles of anger and bitterness, God was able to heal my heart and my soul, although this did not take place instantly. It took some time.

He is telling his father he loves him? How strange is this? I recall, after entering the United States and spending a week in New York during one of our outings, I saw a little boy talk to what I presumed to be his father; however, the little guy looked up to him and said, "I love you."

I was startled and asked my husband, "Who is this person, the man to whom this boy says, 'I love you'?"

My husband laughingly replied, "My goodness, don't you know that this is his father?" At this point, it was beyond my understanding that you told your father, "I love you." I remembered that during our strict upbringing, you never mentioned *love*; you did not tell your parents, "I love you," and it was certainly not reality to me for your parents to tell you, "I love you," either. This was foreign to me.

Another incident which happened the first time I went to church in Birmingham, Alabama. During the offering, the priest would tell the congregation, "Now turn around and tell your neighbor you love them." I thought, *Do what? I don't even know these people, and I am supposed to tell him or her,*

"I love you"? I decided to just tell them, "Nice meeting you." It took some time for me to get this "love business" straight, but it was not until after I got saved and experienced God's love in my life first. Then I also understood that a lot of times you need the love of God to work through you just because you can't love some people on your own.

I hope this helps you to start walking in love. By now, I make sure that I tell my children that I love them every chance I get. I do not want my children to be malnourished or love-starved. I also make it a point to tell my friends that I love them because it has real meaning to me. I might add that I never tell anyone I love them if I don't really mean it. We have to be honest. We can still lend a helping hand to the unlovable as well as walk in love with God's grace. Sometimes, it takes all of God's grace to walk in this kind of love, but God, by the work of the Holy Spirit, will see you through.

Shortly after I was saved and was at home, I was doing what I thought was worshiping the Lord, playing worship music and telling the Lord how much I loved Him when suddenly, the Lord stopped me and unexpectedly gave me deep insight into my heart and soul as if using a huge flashlight and shining it into the darkness of my soul. Immediately, I realized that I was only giving lip service. I immediately repented and told the Lord, "Father, I don't know you as a God of love, only as a God of wrath and judgment. It was at that point that I decided I had to be honest with God myself and let Him know

I actually hated Him for a long time (as though He didn't know that already.) Wow, how gracious God is!

Up to that point, I had become very religious and legalistic and wanted to make sure I prayed and worshiped every day for at least one hour. How foolish because my heart was not in it. Suddenly, I felt like one of the Pharisees. Had I prayed like this because I truly loved the Lord and wanted to just spend my time with Him, that would have been great. I worshipped Him out of duty. However, one day when I started praying, God exposed to me my real feelings.

While praying, I realized that a movie was coming on at 7:00 o'clock, which I desperately wanted to watch, and my prayer hour would interfere with that. I kept looking at the clock so as to not miss the time for the movie. After being honest with the Lord, I felt like a hypocrite and concluded and tearfully said, "Lord, you know what, I am not going to tell you that I love you until I know you as a God of love, and right now, we are going to watch the movie." It turned out to be a love story, and God even ministered to me through the movie. Yes, God is good *all* the time.

God is a *redeemer*. Our Father wants to redeem all our circumstances we have ever encountered or will encounter during our lifetime. What a Heavenly Father! Suppose you are walking in unforgiveness or you are very critical and judgmental toward others, do you think God will still redeem your broken dreams? Absolutely not. As mentioned before, unless you repent and allow God to cleanse and deliver you from any unforgiveness, a root of bitterness will manifest inside of you and build a stronghold in your life. Then guess what? What you have sown, you will reap. Understand that there are *always* consequences.

I know from personal experience that God is a redeemer, and He always has your back. After accepting Jesus Christ as my personal Lord and Savior, God started dealing with me about my deep-seated antagonistic feelings, which I was still carrying with me toward my father. God wanted reconciliation. I certainly did not want to confront my father with the truth— my real feelings toward him. I made a plan for God and told him that I would just call my father and tell him that I am sorry I ever felt angry toward him. To me, that was a good solution, but God had a different plan. Sometimes you must confront your own shortcomings.

Then, much to my dismay, God told me to go home and tell my father in person that I hated him. *Oh, no, God, I can't do that. Besides, I don't have the funds to fly home to Germany.* For me, that was settled.

However, it was not settled with God. When He asks us to do something, He will make a way. Shortly after that, one of my brothers called who did not have a clue about my conversation with God and was at the time at the airport in New York on his way to Germany. He insisted that I needed to go home for a visit, and he would be glad to send the money for the airfare.

Of course, as I wrestled with the decision to have to go home and confront my father, the money came and I no longer had an excuse. While on the plane with feelings of apprehension and fear, God showed me that my father literally laid down his life for his children so that they would have a better and brighter future. I think that was the longest flight I had ever been on; although, I had flown home for a visit prior to that.

Now, the time had come to tell my father. I was literally trembling with fear. What a surprise it was to actually be able to *talk* to my father. It was at that point when God redeemed our relationship. We spend many hours together after that when he shared with me everything he endured during WWII. He especially reminisced about the wonderful friendship with the baroness and what a true friend she had been.

My father had invited me the night before to watch him pray, not so much for his sake, but for mine. As I was sitting there in astonishment how familiar he was with his Heavenly Father and the strong trust he showed, I was amazed. Almost like Moses, he really knew God. I was relieved. Soon, the morning rapidly approached, and it was time for me to come back to the United States. Finally, the time came to say good-bye.

Early the next morning, as I was ready to come back to the United States, I went to say good-bye to my father. He was still in bed. As I was reaching out to him, kissing him on the cheek to tell him good-bye, he affectionately turned toward me and, with a smile on his face, declaring, "Rosemarie, I will not see you again on this earth, but I will see you in heaven," while observing the love in his eyes and a tear flowing down his cheek. That was the first time I had ever seen my father showing any kind of emotion. At that very moment, the most amazing love and peace flooded my heart and soul. The relationship with my father was totally healed. Wow, what a Redeemer we have!

Maybe you will be surrounded by people who are bitter and hateful toward you, or it could be manifested as financial problems or even sickness or disease because you opened the door for Satan to come in and operate in your life. (Of course, there could be numerous other factors involved if you do not get healed, but unforgiveness should be number one on your checklist.) Have you not ever met someone who was unapproachable, or if you did ask them anything, the expression in their faces would just utterly amaze you? Did you ever get the impression they were baptized in pickle juice? I certainly have, but then you never know what they are going through. We should not be offended and try to understand the source of their problem. Could we possibly help or comfort them?

Satan will certainly convince you that you have a *right* to get even, while he withholds the little tidbit of information that you are doomed or headed for destruction. Basically, you are building a fortress, a stronghold that will increase in strength; like a hurricane category 5, it will devastate you and finally kill you, completely wiping you out.

Sure, you ask, "Can I get out of this?" Sure, you can. How? Repent. Turn from it, and God will redeem everything in your life that Satan meant to destroy, but you can't give place to the devil and then ask God to bless you. You choose which master you will serve—God or Satan.

Sometimes, we may hide troublesome things in our hearts that we think are not very significant. But know *all* things in our life are significant and important to our Father. No matter how big your problem or how small. However, remember—it is those "little foxes" that spoil the vine (Song of Solomon 2:15). Maybe you don't get answers to your prayers, or maybe you have problems with your relationships, and you really don't know what the root problem is. It is at this point where you have to examine your heart. Trust me, God will show you if you ask Him.

Not too long ago, I was on a trip to Florida, and while still in Alabama, I heard a grinding noise of my tires. Immediately these thoughts ran through my mind: *Oh no, I can't believe this, my car is breaking down on the Interstate.* I got out of my car, and what I feared came to pass. I stared at my flattened tire, which now resembled a huge pancake.

"Oh God, help. I really need some angels to come and help me," I exclaimed. Confident that my Father was sending help, I walked around the car, opened my trunk, and waited for the "angels" to come.

It was not very long, maybe two to five minutes, when two huge motorcycles approached me and, with smiling faces, inquired, "Do you need some help?"

About that time, another car approached me. A man got out and offered his assistance as well. I told the bikers and the man in the car behind them that I had just asked God to send me some angels, and here they were. They not only exchanged my tires but helped me with better directions, but not without a setback. During their effort to take off the old tire, two bolts broke off and had to be replaced. However, my worries were quickly put to rest because one of the "angels," the man in the car, helped me to go to the right place in Prattville to get them fixed. All I had to do was follow him to an auto repair shop where a maintenance man quickly put two brand-new bolts on my car, and I was on my way again. Isn't God good? I never saw the angels again.

On my way to the Prattville exit, I couldn't help but laugh. You see, I had this mindset about bikers and motorcycles. In my mind, I rationalized that they probably belonged to a gang. What a surprise my Father had for me. I thanked God for sending the angels and noted, "Lord, you are really redeeming everything in my life—even sending the bikers. I repent of having such a negative mindset about bikers." God taught me not to judge a book by its cover. These bikers who came to help me really were angels in a time of need. But when God does something, he redeems with interest. When I finally arrived at the place of my destination in Florida, there was a bikers' convention, and hundreds of motorcycles were not only at the hotel, but every time I turned around, I ran into bikers.

Oh yes, one more thing. God will take the sting out of past hurts. The man who stopped in his car and took me to the auto repair shop reminded me of someone I knew or had known in the past. Surprisingly, his name was that of a person who had disappointed me greatly as a spiritual authority at one time in my life. Even the name had left a bitter taste in my mouth. Although I had forgiven him several years ago, there was still the bad memory of it. I had asked God to heal my memory. He did. Yes, that's right. God redeemed even the name of that person to help me out because I had chosen to forgive him a long time ago (as an act of my will), but now God redeemed the sting of it. God is faithful, and He will heal your wounds if you let Him. Finally, as far as the bikers are concerned, I can honestly say, now I even like motorcycles, and some bikers are actually angels. Praise God.

What is the lesson in this? Sometimes God will show us the light to reveal our blind spots as we travel on our Damascus road and pull us aside to get our attention, just like Paul. He intervenes by His great desire to redeem our "stinking thinking," our way of thinking and acting contrary to God's Word. Therefore, He will let us get stranded on the side of the road. He will shine the light of truth, an eye-opening experience, into the depth of our soul. Sometimes, this shifting will take place on our Damascus road where we find release from ourselves and where God will be able to put the finishing touches on us.

He desires to redeem everything in our lives that was wrong, broken down, or hurtful to us. He is the Redeemer. He wants us to be free without carrying the baggage of past hurts, disappointments, unforgiveness, and any other struggles over which we have had no victory and which are keeping us imprisoned in our own soul. That's when the Redeemer takes over.

Christ is the Redeemer. You know, Christ's crucifixion was during the year of the jubilee. Remember Jesus said, "It is finished." It was at the close of the Day of the Atonement that the jubilee trumpet sounded a release of debts (Leviticus 25:9).

Remember the unfaithful, wicked servant and what happened to him?

And his lord was wroth, and delivered him to the *tormentors,* till he should pay all that was due unto him. So likewise shall my Heavenly Father do also unto you, if ye from your hearts forgive not every one his brother their trespasses. (Matthew 18:34 and 35, *emphasis added*)

The pardon was revoked, and judgment was reinstated. Judgment was revived; the wicked servant was delivered to the tormentors (which are demon spirits) for the payment of his own debt. If you are not meeting the terms of the gospel, then you too will be left open to the law and the tormentors of your soul.

The servant became open game to the reproach and terror of his own conscience, his tormentors, and the demons who were legally able to torment him. Just think, judgment without mercy begets judgment without mercy. "He shall have judgment without mercy, that hath showed no mercy; and mercy rejoiceth against judgment" (James 2:13).

God always allows us to make our own choices, and He will never force you to forgive. However, our choices must be based on the Word of God, and we accept the consequences of our choice. Forgive or do not forgive. Jesus made His choice on the cross at Calvary when He cried out in agony, "Father, forgive them." However, we have to make our choice here on earth as well. Remember, the law is for the lawless. Will you say yes to Jesus and follow Him and receive forgiveness and peace in your soul? Or will you choose Satan and walk into utter darkness of your soul and eventually slip into eternity where eternal hatred and torment prevail?

The Choice Is Yours
Judgment or Mercy?

I pray that you, the reader, will make the choice that will give you life and freedom not only on this earth but for all eternity. Just the small act of forgiveness—only a choice you will make—will loosen you from any bondages or chains that you may be living in right now so that you may enjoy absolute freedom and peace.

Don't let the poison of unforgiveness penetrate your heart and soul. Unforgiveness is like a cancer trying to destroy the quality of your life, but you are free to make the choice to forgive as an act of your will. If you make the right choice, your life will never be the same, and you will be the *winner.*

Admittedly, it will not be easy *until* you make the choice to walk in forgiveness. The hard decision is the choice itself. However, once you get to this point, all the burdens you have been carrying, which were so overwhelming, will fall off your shoulders. Finally, you will be free.

In closing, a word of caution. God will never ask you to come against someone's will. If you are in a situation where you have ministered to and counseled someone and they totally reject your advice, like Jesus said, leave them and wipe the dust of your feet. Anyone who rejects your Godly counsel, forgive them and turn them over to your Heavenly Father as He is the only one who can deal with them. Only He can break through a hardened heart often caused by irreconcilable and horrific situations they have encountered and may require our patience. Sometimes, God will sift such relationships and bring new relationships and at other times, He may restore relationships at a later time. Just ask God for wisdom.

Sadly enough, sometimes even God Himself cannot reach some people because of an unteachable spirit, pride, a narcissistic and power-driven personality, or an antichrist spirit operating through them. God will give you wisdom in these type of circumstances and even take the burden off of your shoulders. Isn't God amazing? His plan for you and for me are good plans.

Yes, God is good—*all the time.*

PERSONAL NOTES

REFERENCES

1. Mike Murdock, *The Winner's Daily Word,* (Dallas: Honor Books, 1984, 22).

2. Murdock, p. 12.

3. S. C. Gwynne, (1998, January). *CRIME: Why So Many Want to Save Her.* (Time, pp. 48–58).

4. *The World Book Dictionary,* 1973 Edition.

5. W. E. Vine, Merrill F. Unger, and William White, Jr., *An Expository Dictionary of Biblical Words* (Nashville: Thomas Nelson, Inc., 1985), Testament, p. 251.

6. *Grolier Multimedia Encyclopedia,* Vers. 10. 0. Computer software. 1-CD Version, 1998 Windows 7 95, Windows 7 3. 1, 1997 8 1997 Grolier Interactive, Inc.

7. W. E. Vine, Merrill F. Unger, and William White, Jr., *An Expository Dictionary of Biblical Words* (Nashville: Thomas Nelson, Inc., 1985), Old Testament, 1984, p. 251.

8. W. E. Vine, Merrill F. Unger, and William White, Jr., *An Expository Dictionary of Biblical Words* (Nashville: Thomas Nelson, Inc., *1985),* Old Testament, 1984, p. 251.

9. W. E. Vine, Merrill F. Unger, and William White, Jr., *An Expository Dictionary of Biblical Words* (Nashville: Thomas Nelson, Inc., 1985), Old Testament, 1984, p. 251.

10. Merriam-Webster Online Dictionary 1. 0 by Gerald Wick. Alan Fincke and Carlyle Potts, 8 1992 Merriam-Webster, Inc.

11. W. E. Vine, Merrill F. Unger, and William White, Jr., *an Expository Dictionary of Biblical Words* (Nashville:

Thomas Nelson, Inc., 1985), New Testament Expository, 1984, p. 250.

12. Black's Law Dictionary, 5t Ed., West Publishing Co. (1979).

13. Vine, p. 251.

14. Robert J. Loescher and Cirlot, J. E., *A Dictionary of Symbols* (1962; repr. 1983); Guenon, Ren, *The Symbolism of the Cross* (1975); Hall, James, *Dictionary of Subjects and Symbols in Art*, 2d rev. ed. (1979); Seymour, William W., *The Cross in Tradition, History and Art* (1898).

15. Vine, p. 535, New Testament Section.

16. Wikipedia, the free encyclopedia (Google)

PHOTOS

Our Home in Germany

My Father, Richard Reinhard

My Mother, Kornelia Reinhard

My Father during WW I

My Father during WW I, Cavalry

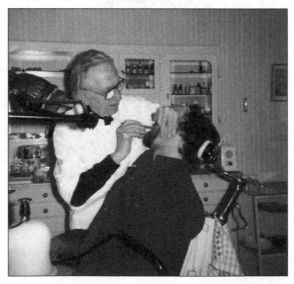

My Father, in his Dental Office

The Baroness

Castle, Schloss Ramholz

Castle, another view

Rosemarie Reinhard Musso during WW II

Rosemarie Reinhard Musso after WW II

My parents during WW II

Rosemarie Reinhard Musso, Immigrating to the USA

Bahnhof across the street of our home

Celebrating my Father's 85ᵗʰ Birthday in Castle

Band playing on father's 85ᵗʰ Birthday at our home

Table Set in Castle on Father's 85th Birthday

**Room in Castle where Band Played on
Father's 85th Birthday**

Belgium Family my Father helped escape during WW II

My siblings before I was born

Family picture during WW II

**Babette-Nanny my Parents took in when
she was six Years old**

My wedding

Mother and sister, Margarita

Mother, Kornelia Weismantel

Sisters are held together by heart strings

My sweet daughters, Barbara and Christine

My sweet daughter, Barbara

My sweet daughter, Christine

My sweet daughters, all grown up